WEST HIGHLAND
WHITE TERRIERS

This game little dog is certainly one of the most attractive of the terrier breeds. With its Scottish heritage of being a tenacious and brave little working dog, the West Highland White is becoming increasingly popular both as a Show Dog and as a household pet. Mrs. Pacey, herself a breeder and judge of international reputation, has written a book for all lovers of the breed, packed with practical advice and expert guidance.

The cover photograph is of Ch. Wolvey Permit.

Courtesy: Thomas Fall

WEST HIGHLAND WHITE TERRIERS

by

MAY PACEY

W. & G. FOYLE LTD
119–125 CHARING CROSS ROAD
LONDON, W.C.2

First published 1963
© *W. & G. Foyle Ltd 1963*

Printed in Great Britain by
Butler & Tanner Ltd, Frome and London

This book is dedicated firstly to my Husband and Daughters who share my love of dogs, and have always been the greatest help to me in running a Kennel; secondly to the many dogs I have owned, both Champions and pets, which have given me so much joy in life.

Acknowledgements

I wish to thank Mr. E. Holland-Buckley, Secretary of the Kennel Club, for his help with the records of the breed, Mr. Dennis Marples for the photograph of Champion Morven, Mrs. Beels, Mrs. Russell, Mrs. Finch, Mrs. Dennis, Mrs. Kirby, Miss Turnbull, Miss Cook and Miss Wright for the use of photographs and pedigrees, all of which have been the greatest help to me in writing this book.

Contents

Illustrations

CHAPTER I

The West Highland White Terrier – Before 1914

I ALWAYS think this dog is so well named; he is one of the oldest Highland Terriers and was kept entirely for his working abilities many years before we knew him as a show dog. In the West Highlands of Scotland he was used for hunting foxes, badgers and wild cats among the rocks and crags of the mountains. To be able to do this it was essential to have a small narrow and very active terrier, full of pluck and courage, who could jump and scramble from rock to rock and also be able to get to the inmost recess of the lair of its quarry. There was no chance of him being dug out, and scratching among the rocks that could not be moved, anything but an agile terrier was likely to stick fast and have his ribs broken.

It was found useful to have a white terrier so that he could be more easily seen among the dark rocks than his sandy, grey and coloured cousins. For this reason he was bred for generations by many of the oldest Scottish families and keepers.

That the breed is of very ancient parentage is proved by the fact that over 300 years ago we hear of James I of England sending to Argyllshire for six little white 'Hearth Doggies' to be sent to France as a present to the King, and to travel in two or more ships lest they should get harmed on the way.

In 1839 came the lovely picture by Sir Edward Landseer, R.A., of sporting dogs; the West Highlander is there too, and also in the well-known picture by the same artist, *Dignity and Impudence*, in which the head study is particularly good, showing the keen and alert expression that is so characteristic of the breed.

We should always feel grateful to Colonel Malcolm of Portallock for bringing this breed before the public. He had a large Kennel of working dogs and loved the breed and thought they should be better known. They were first called Portallock Terriers, and were shown at Edinburgh at that time. I did not see them there, but did so at Crufts in the 'Any Other Variety'. There were five or six of them sitting on benches with big collars and chains and I quite fell for their lovely expressions and character. It was easy to see that it was all something new to them, and they were just taking it and adapting themselves to the unusual. When the breed was registered by the Kennel Club the name West Highland White Terrier was chosen. Two Clubs were formed in about 1905, the West Highland White Terrier Club, which is the oldest, and the West Highland White Terrier Club of England. Both Clubs have worked hard for the breed and now run their own Championship Show each year, drawing big entries.

At the time, good ones were very difficult to get; most of them being bred in Scotland, and the Scottish exhibitors who so well knew the correct type produced most of the winners. A standard of points was drawn up which has since had some alterations.

The Countess of Aberdeen was the first President of the English Club and Colonel Malcolm (who was afterwards President) was Vice-President. Both did much to keep the right type, as there was a tendency at that time to regard the breed as white Scottish Terriers, and breed them with long narrow heads and low cloddy bodies. Fortunately, the West Highland had many staunch friends who worked hard not to lose the right type, keeping their dogs for work as well as show. Mrs. Portman was one of these; her dogs were used for badgers and foxes, and she often arrived at a show with her best dogs all scarred and bitten. She was always very proud of them and a great judge of the breed.

Before the 1914 war the breed was going well with many well-known Kennels and great dogs. I think Champion Morven stood out in the early days as a great show and stud dog.

Mrs. Logan's Champion Runag was a lovely bitch who charmed everyone, and many people came into the breed when they saw her. I still think she could win now, but in those days no dogs were allowed to be trimmed and she was always shown with her real hard coat. Her conformation was excellent and she was a great shower.

Miss Viccars' Champion Kiltie was another great dog, but he went to America for £400; a record price at that time. Champion Dazzler Sands and Champion Glenmohr Model and many other good ones soon followed.

Mrs. Hunter's Champion Morova was a great winner and sired many good ones. Other leading dogs at that time were Mr. W. Baker's Champion Chawston Garry; the Childwich Kennel had many outstanding champions and they were all the same grand type. Many of the best ones were bred in Skye; my first Champion, Wolvey Piper, came from there. Mr. J. Campbell's Ornsay Kennel at North Berwick produced many champions, his Ornsay Bobs was a grand little dog and sired many champions. Unfortunately, he was unable to be shown owing to his tail being damaged.

Mrs. Cameron Heads, whose family for many years had owned and worked the breed, had an excellent Kennel and did much to help to keep the correct type. She did a great deal of winning with her Inverailort dogs.

Mr. Colin Young's Kennel in Scotland produced Champion Morven, and many fine dogs of the correct type and did much to help the breed. So did Colonel and Mrs. Birkin of Nottingham, Mr. Gray and Mr. J. Lee.

Mrs. Cecil Clare has a good Kennel and bought Champion Morven and many other good ones. I had made a start and was doing a lot of winning with a very nice dog—Wolvey MacNab. My first Champion was Champion Wolvey Piper, a lovely dog who had been bred in Skye by that great breeder, Simon McCloud. Miss Rogers had also started with her Gunnersbury Kennel and did so much to help the breed for many years, but the 1914–18 War came and put paid to so many Kennels. All breeding was stopped and food was difficult to get, as no one was allowed to give a dog any food that humans could eat or animals that were producing food. It is difficult to think now that one could not get food. A friend of mine was heavily fined for letting her dog finish a rice pudding. The Police were always around seeing what you were feeding your dogs on. I kept going for quite a time on very bad horse meat, boiled swedes and boiled linseed when I could get it, but the horse meat stopped and I could not go on looking at the dogs I loved and not be able to feed them. I had fifteen put down one day which I have never forgotten and never will. I think in some parts of the country people managed better. Mrs. Lucas was able to keep her Highclere Kennel going and was able to make a good start after the war. Mr. Holland Buckley and his daughter, Mrs. Barber, had a very strong Kennel. He had always been a great help to the breed and helped so much to keep the right type, and after the war he was the first to help the breed going again. I so well remember him writing to me (I was Secretary of the Club then), and telling me to get things on the move. It was not easy, but I did my best.

CHAPTER 2

The Breed Between the Wars

WHEN the 1914–18 War ended, there were few of the old Kennels left and shows took some time to get going again; a 'muzzling' order did not help. Entries were bad for a time, but breeders soon got going, and between the two wars the breed came to its best. There were many great dogs and bitches. Competition was keen, and we were lucky at that time to have a lot of good judges who really knew a West Highlander. Mrs. Lucas' Champion Highclere Rhalet by Champion Moreso was the first great dog and did a great deal for the breed. Many champions were bred in this Kennel in Wales. I think my dog Champion Wolvey Patrician also played his part. He won several Best in Shows and sired many champions. His sons and grand-children had his gift of stamping themselves on any bitch they mated. The Rushmoor Kennel owned by Miss Newall and Miss Smith-Wood was very strong and bred many champions – all a lovely type. I think Champion Rodewick of Rushmoor and litter brother Champion Ray of Rushmoor, both by Patrician, were two of their best. Champion Ray of Rushmoor went to America and did very well there.

The Clint Kennel owned by Mrs. Hewson had some outstanding dogs. I think Champion Clint Cocktail and his sire Clint Crofter, who was by Champion Wolvey Patrician, were both beautiful terriers, but there were many other good Champions in that Kennel as well. Mrs. Allom's Furzefield Kennel was much to the fore. Her Champion Furzefield Patience was her first champion and there have been many others.

Champion Cooden Steeplechaser, Champion Cooden Sapper and Champion Cooden Shrapnel, owned by Mrs. Williams, all made competition strong. The late Mrs. Innes who owned the Bream Kennel was a great supporter of all the shows, and bred many good ones, Champion Bream Glunyieman being her best. Miss Turnbull was showing Champion Leal Stirling and Champion Leal Furry, both great show dogs and sires; also the two lovely bitches – Champion Leal Phoenix and Champion Leal Patricia.

Mrs. Ellis of the Lynwood Kennel produced some lovely champions at this time and still has very good ones. Mrs. Beels' Champion Dude O'Petriburg was another big winner. He was by Clint Crofter and sired some good stock. There were many top dogs and bitches in this Kennel. One of the strongest Kennels was still the Childwick Kennel. Miss Viccars has so many good ones, and it was unfortunate for the breed when she gave them up and went in only for Cairns.

Mr. Railton's White Don sired a lot of good ones. Unfortunately he was born a month after the 'ban' on breeding was put on. Otherwise he would have been a great winner. Mrs. Barber and her Scotia Kennel were winning well; she has now given up showing but is still one of our leading judges. Mr. J. Lee, who was Secretary of the Club for many years, generally had something good in his Maulden Kennel. Miss Rogers who owned the Gunnersbury Kennel also had very nice sound dogs and was a very active member of the Club. Dr. and Mrs. Russell were showing some good Crubens, and Miss Wright, whose Calluna Kennel has produced so many good ones, had that lovely dog Champion Calluna Ruairidh by Champion Ray of Rushmoor, a grandson again of Champion Wolvey Patrician – how this dog did come into the picture. One cannot write this book without mentioning Major and Mrs. McAlester who owned such a strong Kennel in Scotland and bred and showed many good ones. It is nice to know that their son Colonel McAlester is carrying on with the same Prefix, Crivoch.

There were many other strong Kennels in Scotland, and the competition at the Scottish Kennel Club Show held in Edinburgh was always very strong. I think on looking back, we had many more better dogs than we have now. They were all a lovely type; the dogs strong and well made with lovely head and expressions, and the bitches with plenty of substance and full of quality and charm. I think my bitch Champion Wolvey Pintail was most outstanding; I only showed her three times. She won all her classes at the National Terrier Show and was Best in Show, beating some very good Champion dogs of other breeds – it was a great day. Her next show was the L.K.A., at that time held in May, when she again won all she could and was Best in Show. Her third show was the WELKS where she won her final ticket. She was off colour that day or would have won more; she was a joy to show and always did her best for you. My daughter Peggy had trained her to go to ground. She was a great terrier and a very game and good worker who would tackle anything. Her dam, Champion Wolvey Wings, a lovely bitch, belonged to my daughter. She was bred by Miss S. Wood and Miss Newall and was by Champion Wolvey Patrician ex Champion Ruth of Rushmoor. Another great bitch I had was Champion Wolvey Pattern by Champion Wolvey Prefect ex Wolvey Private by Champion Wolvey Poacher. Champion Wolvey Patrician again comes into both sides of her pedigree, but the third generation on the sire's side and fourth generation on the dam's. I first showed her at the Great Joint Terrier Show which was held the day before the L.K.A. She won all her classes and was Best of Breed beating a good champion dog I had who had won the ticket. Next day, at the L.K.A. under the American Judge Mrs. Winant, she went Best of Breed and Best Bitch in the Show after a fight for Best in Show which was won by Lady Howe with one of her celebrated Labradors. She won many Championships and Best of Breed, and Mrs. Winant bought her. The second war was coming and I let her and a wonderful dog, Champion Wolvey Phantom, go. I kept thinking of the first war and not being able to feed them. Champion Wolvey Pattern did very well in America and was the first West Highland White Terrier to win Best in Show at Westminster. It gave me so much joy to read of this great win. Soon afterwards, all dog shows in England stopped and we were back again with food restrictions. I gave many dogs away and sent some to Africa and America, and parted with all my Sealyhams. I just kept a few West Highland White Terriers, hoping to start them again. One was able to get some dog biscuits, and bread was not rationed. Horse meat was not easy, but one could get some every now and then. I learnt then that it was impossible to rear puppies without meat – nothing else can take its place. I had one lovely puppy. My ration – a few ounces of meat a week – was not nearly enough for him but I could do without it.

We had had ten bombs even in our small village. I used to spread the dogs out in various buildings when we got a warning, so that the lot would not be killed at once if we received a direct hit. Some cows were killed but no people. We often had windows blown out and telephone, water and light off. The house dogs, Champion Wings, Cora Ann, a West Highland White Terrier bitch, and the Poodle, Ruby, all let me know a raid was coming before I got the warning from headquarters, and as soon as the telephone went the parrot always called out 'Air Raid warning red' and went and sat at the bottom of her cage. When I had to go out and see what damage was done to report back, Cora Ann always went with me – she longed to catch something. The house was taken over by the Army and Air Force, and my husband and I only had a few rooms. An Army lorry ran over and killed dear Wings whilst she was asleep in the sun in our own drive; just another war casualty!

CHAPTER 3

Progress since 1945

ALL things come to an end and so did the war. It took a little time to get things going. No large all-breed Champion Shows were held, only Specialist ones. The West Highland White Terrier Club held its first at Edinburgh which I judged and was so pleased to find many nice dogs. The West Highland White Terrier Club of England held theirs at Peterborough – so well run by Mr. and Mrs. Beels, with Mrs. Barber judging. It was a great show, and everyone was so pleased to get together again and talk dogs.

Many new Kennels were started. Mrs. Finch made history with her lovely dog, Champion Shiningcliff Simon. He was Best Terrier in Show at Crufts 1950 and Best in Show at Glasgow 1950 – a great win for the breed. Nine Champions were produced from this Kennel and we were all sorry when Mrs. Finch gave up. Miss Wade's Champion Freshney Fiametta, a lovely bitch, won six C.C., was six times Best of Breed, and achieved Best in Show all breeds, Cambridge Champion show 1947. This fine bitch bred American Champion Hookwood Showman and Champion Hookwood Smartie, and was, I believe, the first post-war Champion Dog or Bitch. I always liked her so much, she was well made and a lovely size. I wish we had more like her now.

I think the leading stud dog at that time was Mrs. Allom's Furzefield Piper, a lovely dog of the right type and size. Unfortunately he had an accident and lost a tooth, so judges put him down. He sired Champion Furzefield Pax and Champion Hookwood Mentor, owned by Miss Wade, a lovely dog who sired many champions and won eleven C.C. I think his greatest son was Champion Barrister of Branston, who again sired eleven champions and many with two C.C. He won eight C.C. himself and was always beautifully put down and showed well. His sons have gone on siring champions. The Branston Kennel is always well to the fore and has had 14 champions since the War. Champion Furzefield Pilgrim, also sired by Furzefield Piper, has a long list of champion sons and daughters who have carried on the breed to this present day. To mention two of them, the lovely bitch Champion Slitrig Solitaire, owned by Mrs. Kirby, which was Best of Breed at Crufts 1955 – her dam, Slitrig Sequin, was by Champion Hookwood Mentor, so Furzefield Piper comes in on both sides. My dog Champion Wolvey Pied Piper was also one of his sons – he was a grand little dog and sired me Champion Wolvey Pipers Tune (before he went to America), as well as Champion Wolvey Permit, Champion Wolvey Pickwick and Champion Wolvey Punch. So the line of long established good ones is carried on.

Dr. and Mrs. Russell at this time bred and showed Champion Cruben Dextor by Champion Hookwood Mentor. He was a grand little dog and made history in America, as did their Champion Cruben Moray. This Kennel always turns out something good. Their last champion, Champion Cruben Happy, was Best Bitch at Crufts before leaving for America to join the Clairedale Kennel. Mrs. Beels has had a great run of champions, including her Champion Calluna the Poacher – winner of ten C.C. and ten Best of Breed, a record that speaks for itself. He has also sired several champions. At our last Club show in April 1962, when he was ten years old, he won the stud dog class with a wonderful list of offspring, and was Best Veteran. He was looking so well, and is still a great dog.

Of her two lovely bitches, Champion Phrana O'Petriburg (by Calluna Big Wig, who is by Champion Barrister of Branston) won five Championships before going to Mrs. Chester Caldwell in Honolulu, in whelp to Champion Calluna the Poacher. I hear she arrived safe and well and has had a nice litter. Mrs. Beels' other bitch, Champion Phancy O'Petriburg, has won six C.C.

and was Best of Breed at Crufts in 1962; she is by Phryne O'Petriburg, a son of Champion Barrister of Branston ex Junyer Julie by Champion Nice Fellow of Wynsolot ex Slitrig Sally – she has now retired from the show ring for maternal duties. I am sure she will breed something very worthwhile. Champion Melbourne Matthias was another great stud dog after the war. I think he made up just before shows stopped – he was owned by Mrs. McKinney who has had a long-established Kennel, and was bred by Miss Turnbull.

There are so many good Kennels at the present time, and it is impossible to mention them all. The Kennel Club has kindly let me have a list of all champions which I feel sure readers will find interesting (see Appendix III). Miss Cook's Famecheck Kennel has had a great run of successes. This clever breeder always shows a good type of terrier, and her champions have been many. I think perhaps Champion Famecheck Gay Buccaneer is the most outstanding.

Mrs. Kenney Taylor is another clever breeder; her dogs are always beautifully put down and handled. Her Champion Sollershott Sun Up and Champion Sollershott Soloist are both very gay sound terriers and have done well in the show ring and at stud. Mrs. Barr who owns the Stoneygap Kennels keeps bringing out something good. Mrs. Whitworth has a strong Kennel in the North and is showing very good ones. Her Champion, The Prior of Raventofts, is a very smart little dog. Mrs. Sansom's Champion Quakertown Questionaire and Champion Quakertown Quality are two that she has won well with.

There are many good Kennels in Scotland. The Hon. T. H. Rollo who owns the Kendrum Kennel, has had many champions, and is showing a lovely young dog at present. We do not see Miss Maclean Cowie in the ring very often now, but hope she will soon be in better health and showing again. She is one of our oldest breeders and judges and has had many champions. Miss J. Brown, Mrs. Hays and Miss Herbert all have outstanding Kennels in the North. Mrs. Welch has bred some very good champion bitches. Her Champion Glengyle Tapestry is lovely and she is also breeding good ones. Mrs. Green's Wynsolot Kennel has had some outstanding dogs, which were all beautifully produced and handled by her late husband who we all miss so much at the shows. He was a very kind man and always ready to help the novice.

Mr. Salsbury, who is at present Hon. Secretary of the West Highland White Terrier Club of England, showed with great success the very outstanding bitch, Champion Macconachie Tiena Joy by Champion Shiningcliff Simon, and won twelve C.C. with her.

The breed is very popular and there is a big demand for puppies and show stock in England and abroad. The registration at the Kennel Club was 2,344 in 1961. We get twenty-two Challenge Certificates a year, and these are well spread out. Wales is the only country which has no certificates, and there are a lot of West Highlanders being bred there; so let us hope that Cardiff will once more have them. Fortunately for the breed there are not many very large Kennels, as they are not a dog to be bred on mass. They love people and companionship and need a life where they can develop their brain; they get very unhappy if shut up too much. All my dogs have a lot of exercise and come into the house in turn.

CHAPTER 4

Feeding

Many books have been written on the feeding of dogs, but the principles I myself follow are based on sixty years' experience of breeding.

Different breeds naturally require different feeding, and the West Highlander, being a small dog, wants small amounts of the best available. The adult dog is not a big feeder so I think he should have two meals a day. If the older ones are getting too fat, one meal must be hard biscuit. It is most important that your dog has very good food, and the idea that your pet can live on house scraps is quite wrong – they must have good balanced meals. There are so many different foods you can use: sheep and bullocks' heads, liver and tripe all make a change from horse meat. Well-boiled rice is also a help. It is a good thing to keep plenty of tinned meat in case your supply of horse meat gives out, but I never give it to young puppies, who only have butcher's meat.

When puppies are weaned and have been wormed, they must have five or six feeds a day. I always give Robinson's Barley, made with milk and sugar, as the first meal at 7.30 in the morning. Then:

10 o'clock Savil soaked with meat stock.
12.30 p.m. Scraped raw meat.
3 p.m. Milk meal again.
5.30 p.m. Scrambled eggs.
9 p.m. Nestlé's milk.

I always let them have baked crusts to play with and lots of toys. Puppies must be kept happy. As they grow older, you can give two Savil meals with minced meat added, and less milk meals. I also find boiled hen and rice cooked in the stock a wonderful food for them. I am lucky that we have a poultry farm near and can get large hens, not too old, for 10/-, and also lots of cracked eggs cheap. Weetabix soaked with milk and honey is another change, and chopped-up hard-boiled eggs are also good if a puppy gets tired of other food. Fish also makes a change – I always boil it in milk. At four months the puppy should be having four meals a day and getting on to more solid food. I still give a milk feed at 7.30, but Nestlé's milk is then added to the Robinson's Barley, and minced liver or hearts to the Savil. The raw meat meal is made larger with brown bread crumbs, and for the evening meal I give either custard made with eggs or scrambled egg. One can only feed puppies according to how they are doing, and they may still need an extra feed. I always, from the beginning, use Stress in one feed a day, generally in the raw meat, as they like it best and there is never a crumb left. I also give cod liver oil and let them eat Vetzyme tablets.

When the puppy is six months old and second teeth are through put him on to terrier meal well-soaked with good stock and stale brown bread added, and plenty of meat. He can then have the cooked horse meat, but still give him one feed of butcher's raw meat. Three meals a day should be enough, but if not doing too well give him a milk and eggs meal last thing at night. A puppy at that age has gone through a lot – he has cut all his teeth which a human or a horse take years to do, and must have extra calcium and cod liver oil and the best of food. However, if given too many feeds it may upset his stomach and he will always be emptying himself, which does not help. One has to feed according to the dog, so as to help him grow into a strong healthy specimen.

Feeding a Kennel of about thirty dogs takes some doing. I always have a big stock pot on the kitchen stove at seven o'clock in the morning and a bucket of terrier meal soaked with the stock, which is made of bone and vegetables. The meat is also cooked later on in the day and helps the stock for the next day. Stale brown bread is broken up small and put into the feed when cool, otherwise it will make the meal soggy. All meat is cut up small and added, and all dogs have a very good meal about five o'clock in the evening.

Dogs that you are showing often want more food, since they will lose condition on a long journey before a show, and you must allow for this. Give them what they like best in an extra meal, also cod liver oil. I always find chopped up kidney and beef suet added to a meal puts on flesh, and boiled rice is good. Never let a dog get too thin before you are showing him or he will arrive at the show looking like nothing on earth. When you see all the other dogs looking so wonderful, you just feel your journey is going to be useless; however, at the show, after he has settled down, give him a feed which you have taken with you, consisting of rabbit or chicken and some liver. If judging is not too soon he will look a different dog and you may come home feeling very happy.

In Chapters 7 and 8 I have advised on the feeding of brood bitches and stud dogs. I can only add to this by recommending that you always give your dog the best you can afford. Do not keep more dogs than you can feed really well, otherwise everything will go wrong with your Kennel and you will have many losses and disappointments. Dogs and bitches for breeding have to produce, and it is silly to think they can do this without extra food and care.

CHAPTER 5

Illness

Howevers well your dog or Kennel may seem you must always be on the look-out for any sign of illness. If you suspect that all is not well, take the dog's temperature, and if over 102° send for your vet. It is most important that whatever is the matter should be diagnosed at once and the right treatment given. There are many fatal illnesses that dogs can contract, but if they are inoculated at ten weeks with Epivax-Plus, this gives protection against distemper, hard pad and contagious hepatitis. It is also wise to have an inoculation done a month afterwards against leptospirosis, which is often caught from rats. If not dealt with at once a dog will die very quickly. There are other good makes of inoculation, but I have always used Epivax and found it very good. Although I have had mild cases of hepatitis months after inoculation the dog concerned has always recovered, and not been too ill.

DIARRHŒA can be caused by many things, but is generally due to too much rich food and fatty substances which cause intestinal irritation. A dose of castor oil generally clears up this type of trouble. A serious form of diarrhœa can be the result of streptococcal infection, and if the castor oil has not done the trick, seek your vet's advice at once. A dog often eats grass and vomits up an excess of bile. A tablespoonful of Dinneford's Fluid Magnesia or two Rennies tablets generally puts this right.

HYSTERIA is not a disease. The dog is frightened and barks in a senseless fashion. The cause is incorrect feeding and lack of vitamins and minerals. Get your vet as soon as possible and keep the dog quiet in a dark kennel.

SKIN AILMENTS. For any skin trouble, just give a dose of Milk of Magnesia and a good bath with Kur Mange. If that does not help, a stronger skin dressing must be used, but feed on a light diet so the blood does not get too over-heated.

JAUNDICE is a dreadful thing and may prove fatal if not properly treated. Examine the eyeballs of a suspect patient, and if there is any sign of yellow colouring it is a certainty the dog has the disease. The latter can be caused by a chill on the liver and kidneys which causes disfunction of these organs, or it may be leptospiral jaundice, so do not delay calling in your vet. In the meanwhile withhold all food and drink until he comes and tells you what to do.

EAR CANKER. Fortunately our breed seldom suffers from this painful complaint, but if you see a dog scratching his ear or shaking his head you must examine the ear and clean it out. Then obtain some ear canker powder and blow it into the ear twice daily. Give the dog a dose of Milk of Magnesia as the condition is often caused by over-heated blood.

Every Kennel must keep a small stock of remedies. A blunt-ended thermometer is the most important thing – a dog's normal temperature is 101·4°, but often it will be 102° if the dog is a bit nervous and upset when it is taken. This is nothing to worry about, but if the temperature rises above 102° it is serious.

One must always have plenty of cotton wool in the Kennel, also castor oil, Dettol, Friar's Balsam, Kur Mange, Plufex (for killing fleas and lice), Milk of Magnesia, liquid paraffin, Rennies digestive tablets, glucose, Benbows Dog Mixture (which I have always used with success as a tonic), and Parrish's Food. Cod-liver oil should be in every Kennel. Garlic pills are excellent for any inside upset, Vetzyme yeast tablets have the vitamins that are needed to keep a dog fit, and I have always found them very useful.

With ordinary care, well fed and looked after, a West High-lander is seldom ill or sorry for itself, but the day will come when owing to old age it is kinder to put him down. Be sure you do not forsake him at this time and remember all the pleasure he has given you and the trust he has in you. Consult your vet and he will give the dog an intravenous barbiturate injection in the vein of a front leg. He will be unconscious before the needle is out. An injection into the heart will then be given, and the dog is dead. If you hold the dog yourself he will not be afraid. I never have a horse, dog or cat put down unless I or one of my daughters are there. I feel one owes this to them, and cannot understand people who just send their dog away to be put down. One can well understand their lost feeling waiting for death in a strange place.

CHAPTER 6

Starting a Kennel

As will be seen from the registration figures given in Appendix II, these have gone up from 141 in 1907 to 2,344 in 1961, although the two wars naturally checked progress temporarily. At the present time the breed is on the top of the world and entries are good at the many shows we have. On looking through the registrations in each month's *Kennel Gazette* one cannot help but notice that most of them are by unknown dogs, and a very small proportion by the leading sires of the day, which means that West Highlanders are being bred for the Pet Market, for which there is a very big demand. Many people prefer a bitch puppy, and later on let her have a litter, which often leads to them starting a Kennel. Miss Turnbull tells me she started that way, also Miss Cook. I know that Mrs. Dennis's mother-in-law, who is such an experienced breeder, insisted on her having a West Highlander when she was married, saying no home was right without one. Mrs. Allom's father gave her her first West Highlander as a wedding present. All these pets have led to outstanding Kennels.

I think most Kennels have started this way. The owners have all fallen for the charm of the breed; one gets many letters from people saying the dog they bought twelve or fifteen years ago has died, and they must have another, as no other breed could take its place. West Highlanders certainly make the perfect pet as they adapt themselves so quickly to their new surroundings, very soon one of the family, and are easy dogs to take about. They are also very good with children, but I am very careful that they do not go to very young children unless the parents really understand

dogs, as I should not like a puppy to be at the mercy of a child
who only looked on it as a toy. Many people who have successful
Kennels of other breeds have lately added a West Highland bitch
and are delighted with the breed.

If one is really thinking of starting a Kennel, the best thing is to
buy two very good bitch puppies about the same age. Be sure to
go to a good Kennel for them – do not start with just moderate
ones; the breeder will always help you. If you have two together
they will do better and be easier to look after, also keeping each
other company. Have them in the house as much as possible, but
it is a good thing to get them used to a kennel so that they will
not be upset when they come in season and have to be shut up.
It is not safe to leave them running about at that time; doors can
be left open and a dog come around. If by any chance your bitch
does get served by a mongrel, take her at once to a vet who will
give her an injection – it will be effective if done within twenty-
four hours. Keep the bitch shut up for three weeks as her season
may be prolonged. When your bitches are ready to breed – the
second heat is best – ask advice from the Kennel where you
bought her, and they will give you every help. Starting this way
there is no reason why you should not get well established and
breed some good winners. Do your puppies well and get someone
who knows the breed to pick out the best ones at about eight
weeks old and you can then sell the others, which will help pay
expenses. Have your puppies inoculated against distemper, hard
pad, etc. at ten weeks old. It is a good thing, if you are going to
have a Kennel, and show, to register a Prefix or Affix at the
Kennel Club, which will be a trade mark for your Kennel and
cannot be used by anyone else. Register all your puppies – it is
cheaper to register them if you are the breeder.

Puppies sometimes get their ears up very quickly, others have
them half up and down until their second teeth come through. It
is best to leave them alone as you may do more harm than good,
but if at seven or eight months they are not erect, put the ear
erect, fold in the two sides and with half-inch sticking plaster
wind round the bottom of the ear so that it is erect and standing
straight. Do not use plaster with any elastic in it or it will stop

1. Ch. Morven

2. Wolvey puppies

*A corner of the Kennels
Burbage, 1927*

4. *Ch. Wolvey Patrician*

5. *Ch. Leal Patricia and*
Ch. Leal Phoenix

6. *The Calluna Kennel on*
their natural heath

the circulation and the ear might drop off. Keep the puppy away from the others while this is on or they will be sure to chew it and perhaps damage the ear. Take it off in three days' time and if the ear is still not erect do it again.

I have never found this method to fail, but it may take a little time for the ear to get strong. I always find Parrish's food and cod liver oil helps at this time.

Some people want to start a Kennel by buying winners and all good luck to them, but unless they have great knowledge of dogs and showing, they are far better advised to start in a small way and feel their way. However good a dog may be and no matter what he has won, he can go down if trimmed and shown by a novice who does not know how to do it. Never be afraid to ask advice from those who know, and always call your vet in at once if anything is wrong. You must always do your best for your dogs – they will repay you well.

CHAPTER 7

Breeding

I N your Kennel, the bitches are, if possible, more important than the dogs, but both, of course, have their parts to play. I always try to mate my bitches on their second heat: they should by then be well grown, strong and healthy. To do this often spoils their chances of a show career, and some of my best bitches have never seen the show ring, but they still have a valuable job to do. If they have a litter once a year, there is hardly time to get them in form for shows before it is time to mate them again. One has to make up one's mind what the programme is going to be: make the bitch a champion and then get tempting offers for her from abroad or just keep her at home and look forward to her litter each year.

I have a lovely bitch, Wolvey Peewit, who has bred me a champion each time so far – Champion Wolvey Pavalor in her first litter of eight, and Champion Wolvey Punch in her second litter of seven; since then she has bred another litter of seven, and I have two lovely bitch puppies from it. I look forward to her litter each year more than showing her, and I think it is a good thing to have a bitch or two in your Kennel just to breed from.

I always think the eleventh or twelfth day the best time to mate a bitch; it does not do to mate them too early as they are likely to miss. Be sure and make all arrangements with the owner of the stud dog you have chosen, and also be sure the bitch is ready before bringing her. Bitches are often upset after a long car ride. Be sure she has a good run and does all she should before coming to the dog. Most stud dog owners like the bitch's owner to be there and hold her if necessary, but many say they will come back later – that is all right; one can get on with the job. The bitch is sometimes better without the owner, and some dogs do not like too many people about, especially strangers. The bitch that comes by rail, often a considerable distance, must be carefully looked after. Everything is strange to her and she may be very upset. Get her out of her box into a roomy kennel, with a run that no dog can get either into or out. Leave some water and light feed and let her settle down. A West Highlander soon does so and then you can make friends with her. Examine her, determine when she is ready for service and then proceed. If she has had a long journey it is best to wait twenty-four hours; by then she will be feeling quite at home. If a bitch misses, I always offer her a free service next time she is in season.

The length of gestation is nine weeks and care must be taken of her all the time. I always let bitches in whelp live a normal life for the first month. I then start feeding them on butcher's raw meat twice a day, with a few brown bread crumbs, and a drink of milk at night. I do not give any extra calcium as I find they will get enough from their food. If too much is given the puppies are sometimes over large and the bitch cannot produce them. I have had no trouble with whelping since I have done this, and several bitches have had seven and eight puppies a time – all strong and healthy, giving no trouble at all. I start giving the bitch a teaspoon of liquid paraffin three weeks before she is due and get it up to a tablespoon last thing at night. Be sure and put the bitch in the kennel she is going to whelp in a week before she is due, and keep her very quiet. I exercise them by themselves and let them have as much freedom as possible. Never take them out with a lot of other dogs or they may get hurt and have a dead puppy, which will upset everything when whelping time comes.

You must be sure to prepare the bitch for whelping several days before she is due – cut off all the hair round the teats and examine them to see that they are all normal, also cut the long hair off her behind. Puppies can suck in hair and get very ill, so it is wise not to let them. It is always wise to be there when she starts labouring and watch her carefully. If there is trouble and she has been in labour for more than two hours get your veterinary surgeon at once.

I always take each puppy away and put it on a hot-water bottle in a basket with warm blankets and keep it in the room so that the bitch knows it is there. I find if left on the bitch it will be wet through again when the next one is born, and many puppies die through getting so wet and cold. They come from a very warm place and must be kept warm. If it is a long whelping you may have to give the first puppies a feed. I give glucose and water, just warm, and find this keeps them going until the bitch is ready to take over the litter. When all is over, give the mother a clean bed, a drink of glucose and milk, and let her settle down. She will want feeding every four hours for the first three days – give only milk foods – and then you can get her on to fish cooked with milk, and Brand's Essence of Chicken. She can soon have boiled chicken and rice and then get on to raw meat – eggs are always useful.

The most important thing is to see that all the after-birth comes away with each puppy. It is not always easy but your veterinary surgeon can help with injections after she has finished whelping. A left after-birth can cause a great deal of trouble and send the milk all wrong. Take her temperature twice a day for six days and if she is running one get your veterinary surgeon at once or you may lose the litter. I always have my bitches injected with penicillin twelve hours after they have whelped; it does stop any trouble. However easy the whelping has been there may be some infection there. I think there is nothing nicer than seeing a bitch with her puppies if they are all doing well; there will be no crying, only contented grunts.

If the weather is warm you can get her out two or three times a day for a short time, but do not do so if it is wet with a cold wind blowing, otherwise she may get a bad chill and her milk will go wrong. I always start feeding puppies at three weeks old unless the litter is a small one, and the puppies are doing well. I think it wise to get them feeding as soon as possible in case anything goes wrong. At five weeks old I worm them, keeping the bitch away for several hours. Give the puppies a milk drink one hour after the pill. My veterinary surgeon obtains the pills which are really good. I worm again at eight weeks when the puppies have left their mother, and they then go on to six small feeds a day. See page 23 for feeding chart.

The mother must be taken gradually from the litter. If it is a large one you can take so many puppies away at a time. Never leave the puppies with a bitch that vomits her food for them. After she has left off feeding them, keep her right away from them, letting her play with them once or twice a day. By then they should be making good progress, but be there in case they try to feed. If they are being well fed they will not do so. The bitch who has been having additional food so as to be able to feed her family must now go back to normal. Make sure she is free from any milk, and if not give her a dose of castor oil or Milk of Magnesia and then let her go back to two normal feeds a day.

HOW TO BREED WINNERS

I always find that you have to be careful with West Highland Whites, not to in-breed too much, and if you do be sure the line are all free of nerves. It is no good in-breeding to nervous stock – you must have sound healthy ones. You have, of course, to do a certain amount of in-breeding or you will lose your strain. I always find that a good plan, if you have a nice bitch by a good dog, is to mate her to that dog's grandson out of a daughter of hers. Another recommended way is to mate a bitch to a dog who is by the same sire as herself, but both must have a different bitch line. I do not think father to daughter is normally a good thing though I have done it with great success. I never thought that the resulting stock was as strong and healthy as one likes, although they did me well.

Half brothers and sisters, cousins, aunts and uncles can all come into the picture, but study your pedigrees well before mating a bitch. I write out the pedigree of the future puppies to see if I am breeding back to any faults; the third and fourth generations should be included and taken into account. I always find dogs and bitches throw back to the grand-parents more than to themselves.

Many people bring bitches of quite a different strain to one's top dogs and hope to breed a champion from the mating. This does happen, but not often, and they should breed back again to the original strain to obtain something that will produce high class stock and perhaps the champion they are seeking.

I know that in some breeds, a great deal of in-breeding is done and wonderful stock has been produced, but in some cases a fault has been bred in that is still with them and difficult to breed out. I am glad to think the West Highlander is not being too in-bred, and that we have still the nice hard, healthy little terrier. There are many different Kennels, with established strains, who produce good ones. In Appendix IV are several pedigrees of various strains, and readers are recommended to study them to see how the winning dogs have been bred.

CHAPTER 8

The Stud Dog

WEST HIGHLAND White Terrier stud dogs are very keen and not difficult to manage, but care must be taken that they do not have their first bitch before they are about one year old. And then the first should be an easy mating. I find that if they mate a lot of bitches too young they will not grow on but just tighten up. I think that at fifteen months old they can mate a number of bitches, but be sure the latter are not bad tempered, or the dog may get hurt, in which case you may ruin him for a long time. I wait until dogs are two years old before putting them at public stud, and like to have made them a champion by that time, so that stud work does not upset their show career. You will, of course, have the opportunity of using him in your own Kennel when not too near a show. Dogs at stud must be very well fed, with lots of good meat, and care must be taken that they are not kennelled near any bitches in season, otherwise they will get very upset and lose weight.

I always give a dog a raw egg for his breakfast before mating a bitch and like to get the job done in the morning after he has had a good run, so that it does not upset his normal life. I keep him away from other dogs after the service. Dogs always know when a bitch is about to be mated and are very jealous. Always examine the bitch before the dog sees her, to make sure there are not likely to be any difficulties; nothing upsets a dog more than not being able to mate her. Some older bitches are difficult to mate. I remember Wolvey Padella refusing to let any of my champion dogs serve her, so I put a young dog, Wolvey Piper's

Tune, who had never seen a bitch in season before, to her; she was so surprised that she stood whilst he gave her a good service, and she then bred a nice litter. He is now a champion and one of my best stud dogs. He has sired three champions and many other good ones.

Some bitches are very difficult to mate, and if really bad, it is better not to risk your dog. I had Champion Wolvey Poacher killed in that way. The bitch was not difficult to handle, but when the dog tied she fought to such an extent that he could not get free, was badly ruptured and died soon afterwards – a very great loss. He was such a grand terrier, and one of my best stud dogs; he had sired several champions.

It is best to let the bitch meet the dog when she is on a lead and he is free. Let them play about together and you can then see how things will go. When ready, I put them both on a big table for the service, and obtain the right height for them with folded sacks. If the bitch is difficult, tie her head with a silk stocking; it will not hurt her and you will have more control over her. It is also advisable to have someone holding her. I generally find that as soon as the dog is there she will become quite quiet and you can loosen the stocking. After the service I always hold the bitch's hind legs up, pour a little cold water on her behind to make her contract, and then place her in a dog box for a good rest.

The dog must then be dealt with. Be sure he has gone back all right before going to his kennel, otherwise, if his sheath is doubled back, the organ will swell to a great size and you may have to get a veterinary surgeon to deal with the trouble. If he has this trouble, do not use him again for a fortnight. I once had a dog, Champion Wolvey Chieftain, break a blood vessel during a long service. He came away all right and I was able to get him back but it was at least six months before I could use him again. These are some of the bad things that can happen, but most services, if the bitch is satisfactory, are very easy and no trouble at all. It is always pleasing to hear of good litters by your dogs.

CHAPTER 9

Housing

A LL dogs must be housed well. There are many different types of kennels, but the great thing is their inmates must be kept warm and dry. Our breed is a tough little dog but that does not mean he should have a kennel in the open, exposed to all weathers. I always think that corridor kennels are the best unless you are lucky enough to have a brick building you can convert into kennels and make it how you want. I have had this in the past and how easy everything was. If you have corridor kennels for eight dogs and a table at the end, they are easy to work, especially if you have a good run to it. I always line mine with asbestos sheeting in the kennels and hard-board for the ceiling and sides and have infra-red ray lamps for heating – it is a great help to have electricity in your kennels.

Your puppy kennel must have more heat. I always have thermostatic electric radiators and ray lamps. One must remember that the hook which the lamp hangs on may fall out and set the kennel on fire so it is wise to have two hooks. I never have these lamps on at night unless they have a second hook, only the radiators. I can then sleep feeling that all is well. Paraffin stoves, which I have in some buildings, must be well looked after, and not placed in the kennel with the dog. One must look at them last thing at night and if in any doubt turn them out and give the dogs in that kennel a hot-water bottle – they like that. I find the aluminium ones the best, placed in a stocking and wrapped up in a blanket.

A lot of kennels are required if you keep many dogs, and a

garage is excellent for the purpose. You can put a row of kennels at the back, divide the garage into two runs, and put fencing and gates in front. You then have a kennel and covered run. I always have wooden floors – if cold and wet you can shut the garage doors and the dogs have plenty of room inside. It is a great help to have a large covered run for wet weather.

You must have a quiet kennel in a building for whelping, with a table on which you can examine the bitch if necessary. You must also have isolated kennels, with their own runs and away from all your dogs, for visiting bitches. Kennels and runs must be kept very clean. Puppies will want their's cleaned several times a day; never let them exist in a soiled one.

CHAPTER 10

What to Look for in Your Dog

STANDARD OF POINTS
as adopted by The Kennel Club

GENERAL APPEARANCE

The general appearance of the West Highland White Terrier is that of a small, game, hardy-looking terrier, possessed with no small amount of self-esteem, with a varminty appearance, strongly built, deep in chest and back ribs, level back and powerful quarters on muscular legs, and exhibiting in a marked degree a great combination of strength and activity. Movement should be free, straight and easy all round. In the front, the legs should be freely extended forward by the shoulder. The hind movement should be free, strong and close in under the body, so that when moving off the foot, the body is pushed forward with some force. Stiff, stilted movement behind is very objectionable.

HEAD AND SKULL

The skull should be slightly domed and when gripped across the forehead should present a smooth contour. There should only be a very slight tapering from the skull at the level of the ears to the eyes. The distance from the occiput to the eyes should be slightly greater than the length of the foreface. The head should be thickly coated with hair, and carried at a right angle or less to the axis of the neck. On no account should the head be carried in the extended position. The foreface should gradually taper from the eye to the muzzle. There should be a distinct stop formed by heavy bone ridges, immediately above and slightly overhanging the eye, and a slight indentation between the eyes. The foreface should not dish or fall away quickly below the eyes where it should be well made up. The jaws should be strong and level. The nose must be black, should be fairly large, and forming a smooth contour with the rest of the muzzle. The nose must not project forward giving rise to a snipy appearance.

EYES

Should be widely set apart, medium in size, as dark as possible in colour. Slightly sunk in head, sharp and intelligent, which looking from under the heavy eyebrows imparts a piercing look. Full or light coloured eyes are objectionable.

EARS

Small, erect and carried firmly, terminating in a sharp point. The hair on them should be short, smooth (velvety) and they should not be cut. The ears should be free from any fringe at the top. Round pointed, broad, large and thick ears are very objectionable, also ears too heavily coated with hair.

MOUTH

Should be as broad between the canine teeth as is consistent with the sharp varminty expression demanded. The teeth should be large for the size of the dog, and should articulate in the following manner; the lower canines should lock in front of the upper canines. There should be six teeth between the canines of the upper and lower incisors. The upper incisors should slightly overlap the lower incisors. The inner aspect of the upper incisors being in contact with the outer aspect of the lower incisors. There should be no appreciable space between the incisors when the mouth is closed, ensuring a keen bite; a dead level mouth is not a fault.

NECK

The neck should be sufficiently long to allow the proper set on of head required, muscular and gradually thickening towards the base allowing the neck to merge into nicely sloping shoulders, thus giving freedom of movement.

FOREQUARTERS

The shoulders should be sloped backwards. The shoulder blades should be broad and lie close to the chest wall. The joint formed by the shoulder blade and the upper arm should be placed forward, on account of the obliquity of the shoulder blade, bringing the elbows well in, and allowing the foreleg to move freely, parallel to the axis of the body, like the pendulum of a clock. Forelegs should be short and muscular, straight and thickly covered with short hard hair.

BODY

Compact, level back, loins broad and strong. The chest should be deep and the ribs well arched, in the upper half presenting a flattish side appearance. The back ribs should be of a considerable depth and the distance from the last rib of the quarters as short as is compatible with free movement of the body.

HINDQUARTERS

Strong, muscular and wide across the top. Legs should be short and muscular and sinewy. The thighs very muscular and not too wide apart. The hocks bent and well set in under the body so as to be fairly close to each other when standing, walking or trotting. Cow hocks detract from the general appearance. Straight or weak hocks – both kinds are undesirable and should be guarded against.

FEET

The forefeet are larger than the hind ones, are round, proportionate in size, strong, thickly padded and covered with short hard hair. The hind feet are smaller and thickly padded. The under-surface of the pads of feet and all nails should be preferably black.

TAIL

Five to six inches long, covered with hard hair, no feathers, as straight as possible, carried jauntily, not gay or carried over the back. A long tail is objectionable, and on no account should tails be docked.

COAT

Colour pure white, must be double coated. The outer coat consists of hard hair, about two inches long, free from any curl. The under coat, which resembles fur, is short, soft and close. Open coats are objectionable.

COLOUR

Pure White.

SIZE

Size about eleven inches at the withers.

SCALE OF POINTS

	Value
General appearance and size	20
Coat and Colour	10
Skull	5
Eyes	5
Muzzle and Teeth	15
Ears	5
Neck	5
Body	10
Legs and Feet	10
Tail	5
Movement	10
	100

CONFORMATION

This is most important in the breed, and the Standard of Points of the Kennel Club (see page 41), if closely studied, should help you to know what the West Highland White should look like. I am afraid all dogs do not come up to this standard. There are many with bad hind legs and quarters, and the low-set, bent hock is seldom seen. Too many have straight hind legs and move badly. The shoulders placement is most important, and many fail here, having straight shoulders and neck placed wrong. The dog should have a long neck well let into the shoulders and carry his head proudly. Then, if his hind legs are right, he will be a good mover, a credit to the breed and should do well in the show ring. Heads are another thing that are not too good at the present time, being too narrow in the skull, with eyes set wrongly which spoils the expression. The head and expression of a West Highlander is one of its charms and seldom seen these days. The dark eye is most important and could be better.

Black pads are not taken much notice of in this country or America, but some countries will not have a dog unless all pads and nails are jet black. Our Standard of Points now says that all nails should *preferably* be black. In the old days it said they *must* be black. I remember when judging at Melbourne Royal Show hearing that the West Highland White Terrier Champion Wolvey Pongo, who had gone Best in Show there (a great win) some ten years before I was out there, had been put down at some small show because all his toe nails were not jet black, and this had been upheld, as the dog had not all points correct. I always think the overall appearance of the dog is most important and that the little things do not really matter. Nothing is perfect, but the great thing is to have a well-made dog that can show and look the part, with few things wrong about him.

Mouths are quite good in our breed. The standard does not say how many teeth there should be, only that they should be broad between the canine teeth, and that the teeth should be large for the size of the dog, also that the lower jaw canines of six should lick in behind the upper canines – but a dead level mouth is not a fault. In some countries, what they want is a different story – they must have a full mouth of teeth and count them all, but I must say that in all the countries I have judged in I have never been asked to do this.

Tails should be five or six inches long and carried jauntily, not gay or carried on the back. I would rather see a dog with his tail a bit gay than one who has a low-set one, and does not get it up properly. After all, only five points are allowed for the tail in the Standard of Points so a dog should not be put down too far for this. Tails should not be docked. I can well remember many years ago judging the breed up in the North and finding two with docked tails. The owner was very upset because I put them down. He wrote afterwards to me saying a well-known judge – giving his name – had put them up. This judge happened to be a friend of mine so I told him about it and he said he thought it all right if they had a bit off – he had not read the Standard of Points. Another time a charming couple brought a bitch to be mated, and after she had whelped only one puppy they rang me up in great distress saying they had had a vet to cut off the dew claws and while he was doing this they had taken the bitch for a walk – on returning he had docked the puppy, saying he thought all terriers were docked.

Coats pure white, must be double-coated. Colour is very good in the breed but many dogs are shown without a double coat.

Size of about eleven inches at the withers allows for a good-size terrier, but there are many being shown too small.

CHAPTER 11

Dog Shows

As this book is written to help the novice who has never shown before, the following tips will be useful.

First of all your dog must be registered at the Kennel Club. You will have received a pedigree from the breeder and he may already have registered the dog. If so, you get a signed transfer form from him and send it to the Kennel Club. If not registered, obtain a form from the Kennel Club and get the breeder of the dog and owner of its sire to sign it and send it on with the fee.

You must study the schedule of the show you are going to and keep to the rules. There are many different types of shows, a list of which is given in Chapter 14. However, I always think it is best to take your dog first of all to a small show that has classes for the breed. He recognizes his companions in the ring and so feels at home, but if entered in a large Any Variety Class of all breeds he may be upset and think he does not like shows. He may also become upset when first benched. Everything is so different from being chained up for a short time at home. You must never leave him to begin with, but sit by him and make him feel at home. He will very soon regain confidence and settle down as long as someone he knows is there. You must make him feel it is a day out with you, and I always find dogs love this. They do not mind how long the journey is as long as you are there. I have known many dogs whose show career is finished, howl the place down when their kennel companions are taken to a show and they are left at home.

You have to take quite a lot of equipment with you. You must have a large bag to take all the many things you want – a clean kennel coat, bench blanket, brushes, collar and chain, combs, chalk, towels and always some Vaseline. If your dog does not travel well a little glucose and water may settle his stomach, or if you know he is a bad traveller give him anti-travel sickness tablets. There are many on the market.

All dogs are vetted on arrival, after which you find your bench, – the number will have been sent to you prior to the show. Prepare the bench with blanket and show chair, and place the dog on it, being sure that the chain is short so that he cannot jump off. Dogs have been hung when this precaution has been neglected.

After he has settled take him for a walk, persuade him to empty himself and then clean him up ready for the ring. Put him back on the bench and wait until the judging is going to start. Then give him a brush through, and take him into the ring. The steward will tell you what to do. The judge will place the first five dogs in the order he wants them and the ring stewards will give out the prize cards. If you have won one accept it with a smile. You may be disappointed but never show it; remember there is always another day for a good dog. After the judging put the dog back on the bench, he will feel quite at home there now. If by chance you have won a First, you may be wanted again to compete for a special award, so wait and see. It is always trying for the stewards if a dog is wanted and the owner cannot be found.

CHAPTER 12

Trimming

THIS breed is much more difficult to produce for the show ring than many people think. They must have a hard white double coat and not have all their undercoat taken out, though I have seen many winning dogs with no undercoat. To make the most of the dog and show off his neck and shoulders one has to trim these and blend the coat of the neck and shoulders into the body coat to balance him up. The front must also be trimmed. A good front can look wrong if too much hair is on the legs, and the dog is shown in a high wind or on wet ground. A good judge will look at the bone and not be deceived by this.

It is best to start trimming your dog about six months before you show him, but experts can do it in less time than that. Always keep the coat down and be sure the side coat and on the quarters do not get too full or the dog will look all wrong. I have always found a sharp pen-knife is the best tool; you can work it into the coat as you like, but there are many stripping knives on the market, and a pair of thinning scissors is most useful. Remember you want to show the conformation of the dog in the right way. The West Highlander grows a considerable coat and you must never leave off working on it before a show. If left too long it will suddenly go. You must know your dog and his coat before you can put him into the ring looking his best at the right time.

It is wise to start putting your puppy on the table at ten weeks old and get him used to being brushed; do not overdo it but let him think it is all a game. You can go on and start trimming him gradually when about four months old. By then the coat will have begun to get untidy. Start trimming him at the back of his neck and work down the body, but only for a short time each day or he will get tired of it. You must trim his ears with your fingers and thumb and also trim his tail. It is best to use the thinning scissors on the sides of the neck and chest. Do not take too much off his legs and head, as hair is slow to grow there when a puppy.

As the dog gets older the second coat will start coming through. This should be hard with a good undercoat; keep it tidy all the time and if the puppy coat is very soft take it all off before his second coat comes through. Just leave his legs, head and underneath, then it will grow up level and the sides come through hard. I think a terrier with soft hair on his sides and just a hard section down the middle of the back looks bad. You can again start trimming from the back of the neck down the back and level up the shoulders, tail, head and front, leaving the sides which should now be hard. The great thing is to make the dog look natural and not over trimmed. It is wise to take the coats down on a whelping bitch some time before she is due.

If a coat has blown and is really long it will get very thin. I always take it down with the thinning scissors, leave it about two inches long and then comb it through. Be sure and keep the feet clean and nails cut or filed, but be very careful never to cut the quick – your dog will never forget the experience if you do! If the dew claws have been left on, watch them carefully as they may turn round and grow into the leg. If you see the dog licking them you may be sure they have done this.

Brush the dog every day before a show but do not use the comb too much or you will lose the coat. To clean him before a show, wash his legs, underneath and face, and after the coat is dry rub chalk into it. I find lump chalk is the best, and you can also use some powder for the face and legs. If the ground is wet in the ring put a little Vaseline on his feet and between his front and hind legs – the chalk will stick to it. Be sure he does not go into the ring full of chalk, so after you have rubbed it well in all over the body, take a rough towel, cover him up and pat the chalk out. Then give him a good brush and add a little more chalk in the places that need it. I think it a bad thing when a dog shakes himself and a cloud of chalk springs from him just when he has gone into the ring. Some countries will not allow any whitening in the coat. Judges in England are lenient about this but it is against Kennel Club Rules and one must not overdo it. No judge, after handling a lot of dogs, wants to have his hands and clothes covered with chalk, but I do not think this happens so much as it did. Exhibitors do try to show their dogs clean and white without it, so it is just as a word of advice to the novice that I mention it.

CHAPTER 13

Training Your Dog to Show

A GREAT deal of time and trouble must be taken over this. Start when your dog is about four months old with a soft slip, and get him to walk beside you. Have a bit of liver in your hand, so that he will watch it and keep his head up, and after he has done what you want, give him some – he will soon learn. When he is going really well you can take him out for a short walk, but never very far until he is six months old. Then begin to get him about to meet people and see life. At this age the breed are always very brave. If left until about a year old they may be shy and nervous, not having had an opportunity to develop their brain and seeing only their own home and people.

Take your dog out in a car, into your friend's home and into a town. I always send mine with the Kennel girl by bus into Chichester and let them see life, and after they can walk through Woolworth's with their tails up, I feel they are ready to show. Always have him in the house so that he can meet people there and have the wireless or television on. He will then get used to the loud speakers used at shows, which frighten so many dogs.

When your dog is quite used to the lead, teach him to keep his head up, not smelling the ground but walking well and showing himself off all the time. This is not always easy. Some dogs take a long time to learn, others do it naturally. Teach him to stand with his front straight, head and tail up and ears erect. A little liver in your hand and giving him small pieces will help.

Competition is so strong these days that a dog, however good, will not win unless he makes the most of himself. In spite of all the standard of points eighty per cent really works out on showing. Many a moderate dog has won because he is gay and shows well, while the good one fails because he will not try enough, but I often think dogs are not given enough chance to show. Yours may be the only new one in the ring. You come in, put him straight on to the table and are told to walk him up and down. The dog has not had time to settle down so does not put up a good show. Down he goes without any chance of walking round the ring with the others. When judging, I always give new dogs every chance and have the whole class moved again – you can see much better that way how he compares with the others which have been standing with their head and tail held up and looking their best. Sometimes it takes a few shows for a dog to settle down, and if you have a good one, go on trying – his day will come.

Looking back, I can recall many good dogs not doing the winning they should, but some people give up too soon and say they are unlucky. It is true that showing is expensive and as a result many people only exhibit at shows near their homes. If you want to make your dog a champion you must be prepared to travel and spend money on doing so. You will be lucky, unless you have a super dog, to win three C.C. close at home.

If you make your dog a champion you will feel all the trouble and expense has not been wasted, for it puts a great value on the dog or bitch, and will be a great help to your Kennel. Some well-established kennels will produce and make several champions a year. They know so well how and when to show their dogs, but this book is for the novice who may one day start a Kennel. Everyone has started from the bottom, and I have always found in our breed that breeders are most helpful to the beginner.

CHAPTER 14

The Kennel Club

Dog showing is a nation-wide sport and is governed by a strong committee at the Kennel Club which deals with all things connected with pedigree dogs and shows. This Committee has the Standard of Points for all breeds, and keeps a record of all prizes won by any dog. These wins too are checked to make sure that no dog wins prizes in classes for which he is not eligible. A record is also kept of all pedigree dogs that are sold and transferred to new owners and also of all dogs sent abroad.

The *Kennel Gazette* is published every month, giving details of the meetings of the various Kennel Club Committees, a full list of all dogs that have been registered during the month, transfers and export pedigrees, also a list and dates of forthcoming shows.

If you want any information about a dog, write to the Kennel Club. The Secretary is: Mr. E. Holland Buckley, 1–4 Clarges Street, Piccadilly, London, W.1.

KENNEL CLUB – LIST OF FEES

	£	s.	d.
Registration by Breeder		5	0
Registration by any person other than the Breeder		10	0
Registration (parent or parents unregistered or Breeder's Declaration not signed)	1	0	0
Registration (Obedience Record)	1	0	0
Registration (Pedigree or part pedigree unknown)	5	0	0
Registration (name not changeable) Additional fee		10	0

Re-registration		5	0
Transfer		5	0
Change of Name	2	0	0
Registration of Prefix	3	0	0
Prefix Maintenance Fee		15	0

Holder of Prefixes paying 15s. per annum Maintenance Fee may compound on the payment of £7 7s. After ten annual payments the compounding fee will be £5 5s.

Pedigrees – Three Generations	1	0	0
Five Generations	2	0	0
Export	2	0	0
Export, with special information such as colours, registration numbers, etc. (e.g. France and Germany)	2	10	0
List of Wins (entered in Stud Book)		10	6
Stud Book Entry		10	0
Loan or Use of Bitch	1	0	0
Assumed Name	2	2	0

DEFINITIONS OF CLASSES AT CHAMPIONSHIP AND OTHER OPEN SHOWS

(By kind permission of The Kennel Club)

N.B. – The word DOG includes both sexes.

Wins in Variety Classes do not count for entry in Breed Classes, but when entering for Variety Classes, wins in both Breed and Variety Classes must be counted. A Variety Class is one in which more than one Breed or Variety of a Breed can compete. A First Prize does not include a Special Prize of whatever value.

In estimating the number of prizes won, all wins previous to the midnight preceding the day specified in the schedule for closing entries shall be counted when entering for any class.

Note: In the following definitions, A Challenge Certificate includes any award that counts towards the title of Champion under the rules of any governing body recognized by the Kennel Club.

With these provisos, the following are the definitions of certain classes:

Puppy. For dogs of six and not exceeding twelve calendar months of age on the first day of the show.

Junior. For dogs of six and not exceeding eighteen calendar months of age on the first day of the show.

Maiden. For dogs which have not won a Challenge Certificate or a First Prize of the value of £1 or more (Puppy and Special Puppy Classes excepted).

Novice. For dogs which have not won a Challenge Certificate or three or more First Prizes, each of the value of £1 or more (Puppy and Special Puppy Classes excepted).

Tyro. For dogs which have not won a Challenge Certificate or five or more First Prizes each of the value of £1 or more (Puppy and Special Puppy Classes excepted).

Débutant. For dogs which have not won a Challenge Certificate or a First Prize of the value of £2 or more (Puppy and Special Puppy Classes excepted).

Undergraduate. For dogs which have not won a Challenge Certificate or three or more First Prizes each of the value of £2 or more (Puppy and Special Puppy Classes excepted).

Graduate. For dogs which have not won a Challenge Certificate or four or more First Prizes, each of the value of £2 or more in Graduate, Post Graduate, Minor Limit, Mid Limit, Limit or Open Classes, whether restricted or not.

Post Graduate. For dogs which have not won a Challenge Certificate of five or more First Prizes, each of the value of £2 or more in Post Graduate, Minor Limit, Mid Limit, Limit, or Open Classes, whether restricted or not.

Minor Limit. For dogs which have not won two Challenge Certificates or three or more First Prizes in all, each of the value of £2 or more, in Minor Limit, Mid Limit, Limit and Open Classes, confined to the breed, whether restricted or not, at shows where Challenge Certificates were offered for the Breed.

Mid Limit. For dogs which have not won three Challenge Certificates or five or more First Prizes in all, each of the value of £2 or more, in Mid Limit, Limit and Open Classes, confined to the Breed, whether restricted or not, at shows where Challenge Certificates were offered for the Breed.

Limit. For dogs which have not won three Challenge Certificates under three different Judges or seven or more First Prizes in all, each of the value of £2 or more, in Limit and Open Classes, confined to the Breed, whether restricted or not, at shows where Challenge Certificates were offered for the Breed.

Open. For all dogs. If confined to a Breed or Variety, for all dogs of that Breed or Variety.

Veteran. For dogs of an age specified in the schedule but not less than five years on the first day of the show.

Field Trial. For dogs which have won prizes, Awards of Honour, Diplomas of Merit, or Certificates of Merit in actual competition at a recognized Field Trial.

Brace. For two exhibits (either sex or mixed) of one Breed or Variety belonging to the same exhibitor, each exhibit having been entered in some class other than Brace or Team.

Team. For three or more exhibits (either sex or mixed) of one Breed or Variety belonging to the same exhibitor, each exhibit having been entered in some class other than Brace or Team.

Foreign Dogs. For dogs of any Breed or Variety of foreign extraction not classified in the Kennel Club Regulations for Classification and Registration.

Sweepstake Class. For Brace, Team, Stud Dog, Brood Bitch, Veteran and Breeders Classes only, in which the entry fees may be given as prize money in such proportion as the Committee of the Show may determine.

Subject to the above, and to any Regulations, Show Committees may offer such prizes and make such classification and definitions thereof, as they think fit, except that:

(a) All classes advertised in the schedule of the Show must be clearly defined in the schedule, in accordance with the Kennel Club Show Regulations.

(b) If any class be provided with a definition other than those defined above, the word 'Special' must precede the name of such Class.

(c) The words Grand, Champion, or Challenge, must not be used in the designation of any Class or Prize for which an entrance fee is charged and for which entry has to be made prior to the day of the Show.

(d) No Field Trial Class other than that defined above shall be permitted.

The following extracts from Kennel Club Show Regulations may be noted:

A dog may not compete in any Variety Class or for a prize for best Dog in Show, Best of Either Sex in Show, or Best of any Specified Grouping of Breeds, unless it has competed in a Class for its breed open to all exhibitors if a Class for which it is eligible is provided.

Best in Show Competition. (a) All reasonable steps will be taken to warn exhibitors to bring their dogs into the ring for the judging of Best in Show, etc., but the Committee cannot be held responsible for absentees from these competitions.

(b) The dogs eligible to compete for Best in Show are:

Those awarded Best of Breed provided that they have not been beaten in a Variety Class.

DOG SHOWS

EXEMPTION SHOWS. These are the smallest shows held but there is no separate classification for individual breeds. Four classes are permitted for pedigree dogs and there are usually others for mongrels and cross breeds. Included under this heading are humorous classes, such as 'The dog most like its owner', 'The fattest dog', 'Dog with most soulful eyes', etc. These shows are usually held in conjunction with fêtes or flower shows, and in aid of some charity.

These are the only shows where registration at the Kennel Club is not a necessity before the dog is shown and where registered and unregistered, pedigree and mongrel, can be shown together. They make an excellent first show for puppies to accustom them to the proximity of other dogs of different breeds. As the show only lasts two or three hours the puppies do not get tired. Entry fees are small, between 1s and 2s. 6d., and entries are made at the show.

SANCTION SHOWS. These are the smallest of the 'real' dog shows held under Kennel Club show regulations, and must not exceed twenty classes. These shows must not commence before 5 p.m. except on Saturdays, when they may start at 12.30 p.m. The first prize is often 10/– and the entry fee 2/6d. per class. Only members of the club, association or society holding the show may compete. Membership is usually open to anyone who pays a small membership fee.

Challenge certificate winners may not compete at sanction or limited shows, nor may dogs that have won more than four first prizes each to the value of 20/– or more in post graduate, minor limit, mid limit, limit and open classes. These are good shows for the novice owner and novice dog, as there is no specified time for the close of the show. Exhibits may be taken home whenever the owner wishes.

LIMITED SHOWS. Limited to the members of clubs, associations or societies, or to residents within a specified area. Neither of the above types of shows are 'benched', i.e. have rows of pens provided in which the dogs sit so that they may be viewed by visitors to the show. Sometimes benches are provided at limited events and then a benching fee is charged additional to the entry fee. One bench fee is charged for each dog, however many classes it may be entered in.

Challenge certificate winners may not compete, but the quality of the entrants is usually much higher than at the smaller sanction shows. Some classes are usually provided for separate breeds.

OPEN SHOWS are, as the name implies, open to all comers, and are those at which there is no restriction as to the exhibitor making entries in the classes provided. Champions are often entered in the open classes at these shows, and competition is very keen. If the beginner really wishes to compare his dog with good specimens of the breed, and see terriers prepared and shown to advantage, exhibit at any open show, entering in the first classes scheduled for the breed. It is usual to see some really good exhibits at open shows.

Benches are usually provided; the various breeds scheduled have their benches together, consecutively numbered.

Open shows start much earlier in the day, judging commencing about 11 to 11.30 a.m. The time that dogs may be removed from the show is printed in the schedule, and it is a strictly enforced. Kennel Club rule is that all dogs must remain at the show until this hour.

Prize money is higher: £1, 10/-, 5/-, for 1st, 2nd and 3rd, with a prize card for the reserve or 4th. Entry fees are higher, too, 5/- or 6/-, plus a bench fee of 2/6d. or 3/- for each exhibit. At all benched shows exhibits must remain on their benches except when they are being shown or for short periods when they are being exercised.

CHAMPIONSHIP SHOWS are similar to open shows, but are those shows at which the Kennel Club Challenge Certificates are offered. These are the largest and most important events of the canine world.

The National Terrier Club holds an annual championship show. This, as the name implies, is for all breeds of terriers. This great show is held in aid of the Animal Health Trust.

The general championship shows cater for many breeds. There are twenty-one of these shows each year. The largest, and in fact the largest and most important show in the world, is that known to everyone as 'Crufts'. This show, which was started by the late Mr. Charles Cruft as a profit-making concern, was taken over on his death by the Kennel Club. It is now held instead of the show which took place in November in pre-1939 days as the Kennel Club Championship Show.

Prize money at the championship shows is £2, £1, and 10/-, and entry fees vary from show to show from 10/- to as much as 20/-, with a benching fee of from 3/- per exhibit.

It must be realized by exhibitors that these shows incur heavy expenses in their production. The summer outdoor shows with the necessity of providing vast marquees for benching the dogs in comfort and provide cover for the judging rings in case of rain, incur very large liabilities for this alone.

The shows held during the colder months of the year must be held in a heated hall for the comfort of exhibits, exhibitors and general public. Venues of sufficient size for the great championship shows 'cost the earth' to hire, and this is but one of the many expenses that must be met by the Society running the show, hence the seemingly high entry fees.

In many other countries no prize money is offered at dog shows, only medals and souvenirs, prize cards and ribbons.

CHAPTER 15

Judging

THE day may come when you are asked to judge for the first time. Do not accept unless you feel you can do it, but everyone has to make a start. You may feel rather nervous about it, but when you get into the ring, you will be so interested that everything else will be forgotten. Whatever you do, judge the dogs as *you* think and not just follow other judges' awards. Have your dogs moved round the ring and watch carefully how they move – dogs with well placed shoulders will move with a good stride, straight shouldered ones move with little short steps. Go over them carefully on the table and have them moved up and down – this is very important. I generally find that when they first move round the ring you can spot your winner unless he or she has a bad mouth or eye. Do not be afraid of putting them in the order you want, and how you have judged will show your knowledge of the breed and help to make your name as a future Championship Show Judge.

Never talk about what you are going to do beforehand. I have so often heard in the past novice judges saying what they are going to do when they get into the ring. How wrong they are. You must go into the ring with an open mind, and judge the dogs that come before you as they show on the day. If you do this you will not go far wrong. You must study the standard of points laid down by the Kennel Club and get a clear picture in your mind of the value of them all, so that you can judge a dog all through and not be carried away by one thing wrong. If you have difficult decisions to make do not hurry over them; make sure of your winners and then put them up. Do not keep going back and changing them round after you have once placed them. I have found in our breed that judges do their best, but some, of course, have more knowledge than others. Everyone has to learn, and experience is the great thing.

7. *Int. Ch. Cruben Dextor*

8. *Ch. Shiningcliff Simon, Best Terrier at Crufts, 1950*

Ch. Barrister of Branston

Photo: Thurse

10. *Ch. Wolvey Punch*

Photo: Fall

Photo: Shafer

11. Eng. & Am. Ch. Fame Check
Lucky Charm

Photo: Fall

12. Furzefield Piper

13. Ch. Sollershot Solois

Photo: Cooke

14. Ch. Slitrig Solitaire

CHAPTER 16

How I Started

AFTER I was married in 1910, I wanted a small breed. I had had a large Kennel of poodles, greyhounds and a few whippets. I kept some of each breed and, remembering the West Highland White Terrier I had seen at Crufts, thought that was the breed I wanted. I asked the late Jack Holgate, whom I still think is the greatest judge I have ever known, to get me a good bitch. He said, 'You are asking me something and you will have to wait.' He sent me a lovely bitch which I registered as Wolvey Frolic. I showed her at Taunton Champion Show and won some second prizes with her. Everyone asked me where I got her from. She was a grand-daughter of Champion Morven on both sides of her pedigree, but she caught distemper, and after weeks of nursing died. At that time there was nothing to give dogs against disease. How lucky we are now with all the injections for distemper and other dog diseases. I can remember later on losing thirty dogs or more at a time in a bad epidemic. I sometimes look back at photographs of lovely dogs I had who died of the disease. West Highlanders are great fighters and do not die easily. It was generally after many weeks of nursing, day and night, that they either died or recovered – often being left with bad teeth or corah. Many times one felt one could not go on, but my motto has been 'never give up' and so I always went on.

My next buy was a bitch, Wolvey Thistle by Inverailort Roy – she was a charming bitch. My husband and I went to Mill Hill and bought her from Mr. Trevena, together with a very promising dog puppy. The next day we lost her! She had got through the fencing in the garden and just gone over the Downs. We did all we could to trace her, and had a report of her in some woods ten miles away. I felt that was 'Good-bye' to another lovely bitch. The next day I was looking over the Downs when I thought I saw a hare. I was not sure so I took another terrier with me to see what it was. To my delight it was my bitch sitting there – just thinking. She followed the dog I had and came home; what a relief. She settled down and bred me some good stock and did quite a lot of winning.

The late Mr. Holland-Buckley who was always such a good friend let me have the Chiel; this dog was litter brother to Champion Morova but his colour was not too good, although he was a grand dog in every way and sired many winners. I sold him to the Hon. Mrs. Portman who wanted him to join her pack of working terriers and go to ground. He did very well – he was a real terrier.

By this time, I had quite a good Kennel of the right type, and went ahead. I had bought a very nice dog who afterwards I made a Champion; my first Champion Wolvey Piper. He was bred in Skye and was a genuine West Highland White Terrier. My next Champion was Champion Wolvey Rhoda. I saw her among several puppies in a dog shop in Bond Street. I thought her so lovely I had to have her at eight weeks old. She was a delightful bitch and went to America with Champion Wolvey Piper during the 1914–18 War. I heard she had done great things and did a lot of travelling. I was only so sorry I could not have kept her to breed from.

Life and dogs went on. After the 1914–18 War, having had most of my Kennel put down, I was very short of stock. Mr. J. Campbell advertised he was giving up the Ornsay West Highlanders and only going on with his celebrated Scotties. I went up to North Berwick with strict instructions from my husband that I must not buy more than one, or two at the most. I bought six and broke the news to him by wiring, 'Send a lorry to meet me at Leicester.' Unfortunately, I had bought a young puppy which developed distemper very soon and I lost all the lovely bitches but saved two dogs, one of which became Champion Wolvey Chieftain. He took a long time to get right, but was a really nice dog and did me well.

I went on showing and breeding, but my great success came with a bitch, Champion Wolvey Clover, which Mr. J. Campbell sent me with her sister when young puppies. Mrs. Spottiswoode had the sister and she helped to make her Kennel. Clover bred me Champion Wolvey Patrician which I still think the best West Highland White Terrier I have had – he had a charmed life. I had an old man as Kennel Man at that time. He sent word to me that the bitch had whelped in the night, which was before her time. I went out and he said there were two dead puppies in the barrow, the others being all right. I took the two puppies into the house and worked on them. After a long time the dog came round and he went on and did well – he was Patrician.

We had another bad outbreak of distemper when they were about six months old and dogs were dying every day. Patrician caught it very badly and began having dreadful fits. At that time when they had fits the end was in sight. I could not let this dog die and put him in a dark kennel and fed him on milk and bromide; like all mental cases, the dog always drinks. For six weeks this went on – most of the time he was unconscious. Finally he came to. It took months to get him right, but what joy it gave me when he won his first certificate and afterwards made history in the breed as a Sire and Best in Show winner. He was a brave dog, rather self-willed, and he hated being in a small ring. He obviously thought that walking a few yards just to turn back again was silly. I always showed him in the big ring on a long lead – he used to wait till the end of the lead was tight – I looked the other way, and away he came looking his best. He was a dog I shall always remember and love.

His litter brother Champion Wolvey Patrol was quite different, being a gay tough little dog. Together they won The Dr. Sydney Turner Shield for Best Brace in Show at the Kennel Club Show, having been first and second in the Open Class of the breed. The braces were judged in groups. They won a strong terrier brace before winning the final. It was a great day for the breed. Patrician, which really established my strain, was by

Champion Wolvey Guy, a dog I had bought as a puppy and which did so well for me. I always feel I owe most to the late John Campbell of North Berwick who helped me so much and let me have such good bitches. Champion Wolvey Skylark, Champion Wolvey Clover and Champion Wolvey Fanny were only some of them.

I went on trying to get the perfect West Highlander. I always tried to keep the correct type and improve the conformation which was not too good in those far-off days. I also always let my dogs have every opportunity to work, and I know they have never lost their courage. I well remember many years ago when we lived at Burbage. The Atherston Hounds lost a fox in our garden. After they had left I let out two West Highlanders. They soon found him under some pea sticks in the kitchen garden and away they went. At one time all our dogs were worked and how they enjoyed it. Today, rats are the only quarry they have, and how quick they are on to them.

No terrier should just be a show dog. True, they have their ring career and have to be kept right for it, but afterwards they should live a natural life. I never show my dogs very much because of this – four or five Championships is enough for me, and the dogs then become just happy everyday dogs. My daughter, Peggy, has a farm in Oxfordshire and I can send them up there for a change. I feel so strongly that they should have every chance to work and keep happy and active. Just to live in Kennels is very dull for such a game terrier. During the fifty-two years I have been breeding them I have had many great champions and many wonderful pets.

CHAPTER 17

The West Highland Abroad

Aas one would imagine there is a considerable demand for such
an attractive terrier, and West Highland Whites have gone
to most places in the world where dog shows are held. America
has always bought a great many of our best, and in 1962 a West
Highland White Terrier imported from England, American
Champion Elfinbrook Simon, owned by Miss B. Worcester, won
Best in Show at Westminster. He was exported by Mr. L. Pearson,
who, when a professional handler in our breed, made so many
champions. Now he has retired and is judging and awarding
champions in many breeds.

This was the second time a West Highland White Terrier
achieved such success at Westminster. Champion Wolvey Pattern
had this honour when owned by Mrs. J. Winant, who both before
the War and afterwards had such a strong Kennel and imported
many top dogs. Mrs. Mellon and Miss B. Worcester have also
imported many champions and the late Mrs. C. Dixon, a great
lover of the breed, who had the Clairedale prefix, did a great deal
of winning with imported stock, and also with their progeny. I
am glad to know her daughter, Mrs. Newcombe, is carrying on
with them, although her chief breed is whippets.

I had the honour of judging West Highland White Terriers at
the Specialist Show in New York in 1955, and was very impressed
with their quality. They were a nice type, well shown and pre-
sented and not too small. The exhibitors were all so sporting and I
very much enjoyed it all. I always hope on my trips abroad to see
some West Highland White Terriers, and in 1961 I had a very

nice entry of them at Stockholm. The Best of Breed was a really lovely bitch, Champion Snow Flake. I would like to have taken her home with me; she was Swedish bred by International Champion MacMahons Vickie Vire. The winning dog was Lasara Lennie, imported by Mrs. Graham and Mrs. Hazell. He looked and showed well.

When I was in Tasmania and judging a large Any Variety Class, a very nice West Highlander came in. I liked him very much and was able to award him several prizes. I also had quite a few to judge at Melbourne Royal but the standard was not quite so high. However, I hear that quite a number have been sent out since, which should help the breed.

I have judged and seen the breed in Holland, France and other countries, and the winners have generally come from England. They are a breed that do well in all climates, but many people do not know how to deal with their coats, and often a good dog does not do well because of this. In most countries they are well put down and I have seen a great improvement in the last few years. Everyone abroad loves the breed, and they are very popular as pets and companions. There are a fair number being exported all the time, but, breeders, be sure and send out good ones, which are not shy but will show well, so as to uphold the good name of the breed. We do not want them to get the reputation of being nervous. A long flight, a strange country and people, are enough to upset most dogs, but if they are game they will settle down satisfactorily.

EXPORTING DOGS

One receives many enquiries from abroad for dogs, but I always feel you must find out first what sort of country they are going to and for what they are wanted. You can often tell from the letter received, but never just send a dog off into the unknown. Australia has two months' quarantine and dogs can only go there by sea at the present time. This means a very long, trying time for them, so do not send a bitch in whelp. By aeroplane it is easy to get dogs to most countries quickly these days. Be sure and go to a good firm to export your dog – they will deal with the many papers and forms which have to be filled up, and will see that your dog gets on to the plane.

If it is a dog you are exporting, you have to get a vet's certificate to say that both testicles are correct. Then transfer the dog to the new owner and obtain an Export Pedigree from the Kennel Club. A few days before departure get a vet's certificate to say the dog or dogs are healthy and have not been in contact with any infectious diseases. If going on a long flight, you must send plenty of food for the journey. I always send minced cooked meat, hard boiled eggs, Nestlé's milk, Brand's Essence and hard biscuits – and always include a food bowl, tin opener and full directions for feeding. If going by boat you can arrange for your export agent to supply the food. You will have to pay extra for this, and they will then supply what you specify. It is no good relying on the ship's cook to give the correct food, and if not fed properly the dog will arrive in a sorry state. In some ships dogs are wonderfully looked after, but others are not so good – it depends if there are dog lovers on board.

To send to Sweden you have to have a blood test taken from the dog a few days before departure. Your vet will see to this for you, and also fill up the forms. Be sure your dog is very fit before he goes, and never send a shy one. Always let the new owner know in good time what plane or ship is being used and ask him to cable you on arrival. One is always anxious until news comes that all is well.

CHAPTER 18

Looking to the Future

WHAT will it be – atom bombs or dog shows? Naturally we all hope the latter. Certainly the West Highland White is a great breed, and is now doing so well. We have at the present time many people coming into it, all very keen to do their best. Many Kennels who only started a few years ago are producing champions and showing them well. The West Highland White Terrier people are a nice crowd and all out to help the breed and each other. You seldom hear a word of complaint at a judge's award, whatever they may be feeling. If anyone is in trouble and wants help they will rally round.

I well remember after the last war and just when shows had started again, being very ill and in bed for one and a half years. It took some time to get on my legs again – how kind everyone was. All said the Wolvey Kennel must go on, and the offers of help I shall never forget. The late Arthur Wade, the great West Highland handler, offered to take all my dogs free of charge. Miss Wright offered to come over twice a week to cut up dog meat and help in any way – though petrol was rationed. So many people spent their ration points on sending me parcels, and petrol on coming to see me. It is no wonder I have the greatest affection for them all, and always try my best to help them and the breed in every way.

I feel that with such a grand lot of breeders and exhibitors there is nothing to worry about in the future, and I only hope they keep to the right type and size. I should hate to hear this breed described as 'Min. Westies'. I do not think the name 'Westies' describes our breed – it sounds like something very soft. The West

Highland White Terrier is its correct name and I hope all breeders will bear this in mind in their breeding programmes and remember the words of the late Mr. Holland-Buckley in his book on the breed – 'Breed them hardy and breed them game that they may ever uphold the reputation of their ancient home, the West Highlands of Scotland.'

APPENDIX I

Breed Clubs

There are two Clubs for this breed:

THE WEST HIGHLAND WHITE TERRIER CLUB,
Secretary: Mr. E. Hay,
Broomhouse,
Berwick-on-Tweed.

and the

WEST HIGHLAND WHITE TERRIER CLUB OF ENGLAND
Secretary: Mr. Salsbury,
231 Derby Road,
Long Eaton,
Notts.

Both Clubs will do their best to help you.

List of Registrations from 1907 to 1962

(showing the rise in popularity of the breed)

1907 – 141	1926 – 348	1945 – 675
1908 – 249	1927 – 327	1946 – 1,017
1909 – 351	1928 – 347	1947 – 1,056
1910 – 442	1929 – 350	1948 – 1,114
1911 – 583	1930 – 345	1949 – 1,193
1912 – 596	1931 – 261	1950 – 1,018
1913 – 631	1932 – 267	1951 – 992
1914 – 522	1933 – 598	1952 – 968
1915 – 239	1934 – 628	1953 – 895
1916 – 193	1935 – 718	1954 – 948
1917 – 97	1936 – 757	1955 – 1,080
1918 – 55	1937 – 682	1956 – 1,327
1919 – 126	1938 – 633	1957 – 1,263
1920 – 244	1939 – 424	1958 – 1,448
1921 – 371	1940 – 138	1959 – 1,785
1922 – 499	1941 – 135	1960 – 2,070
1923 – 587	1942 – 175	1961 – 2,344
1924 – 688	1943 – 277	1962 – 2,614
1925 – 372	1944 – 494	

List of Champions from 1907 to 1962

Name	Owner
	1907–1939

1907
Morven	Mr. C. Young
Oransay	Countess of Aberdeen
Cromar Snowflake	Countess of Aberdeen

1909
| Keltie | Mr. C. Viccars |

1910
| Runag | Mrs. M. A. Logan |
| Pure Gem | Mr. J. B. Hamilton |

1911
| Cairn Nevis | Mr. J. B. Hamilton |
| Lagavulin | Messrs. Cleare & Buckley |

1912
Cairn Ransa	Mr. C. Clare
Morova	Mrs. M. S. Hunter
Scotia Chief	Miss W. Buckley
Blantyre Minnie	Mrs. P. Birkin
Swaites Cruachan	Mrs. L. Portman

1913
| Kilree Bag o' Tricks | Miss D. M. Sharpe |
| Rosalie of Childwick | Mr. C. Viccars |

1914
Lothian Defender	Miss F. Mackenzie
Moreso	Mrs. B. Lucas
Mountaineer	Mr. J. Lee
Glenmhor Guanag	Mr. C. Viccars
Maulden Creena	Mr. J. Lee

1915
Hyskear of Childwick	Mr. C. Viccars
Ornsay Defender	Mr. W. T. Glaisby
Repton Rollick	Mr. G. Renwick
Chatty of Childwick	Mr. C. Viccars

1916
Wolvey Piper	Mrs. C. Pacey
Wolvey Rhoda	Mrs. C. Pacey
1917–19 No Awards	

Name	*Owner*
1920	
Charming of Childwick	Mr. C. Viccars
Highclere Rhalet	Mr. B. Lucas
Highclere Romp	Mrs. B. Lucas
White Sylph	Mr. J. H. Railton
Wolvey Skylark	Mrs. C. Pacey
1921	
Chum of Childwick	Mr. C. Viccars
Craig Witch	Mrs. C. M. Bird
Highclere Roamer	Mrs. B. Lucas
1922	
Barlae Perfection	Mr. W. Prentice
Gwern Wilfred	Mrs. E. H. Spottiswoode
Wolvey Chieftain	Mrs. C. Pacey
Wolvey Jean	Mrs. C. Pacey
Wolvey Perseus	Mrs. C. Pacey
1923	
Gwern Remembrance	Mrs. E. H. Spottiswoode
Harviestoun Mab	Mr. J. E. Kerr
Highclere Rescuer	Mrs. B. Lucas
Maulden Miranda	Mrs. E. H. Spottiswoode
Wolvey Fanny	Mrs. C. Pacey
Wolvey Vida	Mrs. C. Pacey
Wolvey Clover	Mrs. C. Pacey
1924	
Chiel of Childwick	Mr. A. J. Warren
White Sylvia	Miss I. Buckley
Wolvey Guy	Mrs. C. Pacey
1925	
Alpha of Gunthorpe	Mrs. E. H. Spottiswoode
Crivoch Cadet	Major W. H. S. McAlester
Culprit of Gunnersbury	Miss H. W. Rogers
Ornsay Sporran	Mr. J. Campbell
White Smasher	Mrs. C. Pacey
Wolvey Witch	Mrs. C. Pacey
1926	
Cooden Sapper	Mrs. O. R. Williams
Cooden Suzanne	Mrs. O. R. Williams
Crivoch Cheery	Major W. H. S. McAlester
Furzefield Patience	Mrs. D. P. Allom
Little Dusty	Miss E. Eccles
Wolvey Patrician	Mrs. C. Pacey
Wolvey Patron	Mrs. C. Pacey
1927	
Cooden Swankpot	Mrs. O. R. Williams
Crivoch Candida	Misses B. M. Sanger
Dornie Busybody	Mrs. C. Pacey

Name	*Owner*
1927—*cont.*	
Gwern Dwynwen	Mrs. E. H. Spottiswoode
Wolvey Patrol	Mrs. C. Pacey
Wolvey Wish	Mrs. C. Pacey
1928	
Betsy MacPherson	Miss M. Davidson
Cooden Safety	Mrs. D. P. Allom
Kilfinichen Kirsty	Miss E. J. McVean
Moses of Daneend	Messrs. E. R. Porch & F. E. Todd
Ophir Chiel	Mrs. A. J. Warren
Ophir Nancy	Mrs. A. J. Warren
1929	
Carlin Melvich	Mrs. E. M. Mackay
Elmslea Reyna	Miss M. P. Featherstone
Fidus Flos	Mrs. C. Pacey
Gay Lad of Alard	Mrs. H. M. Baker
Leal Heatherbell	Miss M. Turnbull
Ophir Rowdy	Mrs. A. J. Warren
Placemore Caution	Mrs. A. W. Bird
Ray of Rushmoor	Miss V. M. Smith-Wood
Rita of Rushmoor	Miss V. M. Smith-Wood
1930	
Cooden Shrapnel	Mrs. O. R. Williams
Cooden Stonechat	Mms. A. W. Bird & D. P. Allom
Ruth of Rushmoor	Miss V. M. Smith-Wood
Wolvey Pauline	Mrs. C. Pacey
Wolvey Pepper	Mrs. C. Pacey
1931	
Clint Cocktail	Mrs. B. Hewson
Cooden Steeplechaser	Mrs. O. R. Williams
Cooden Sunita	Mr. R. W. Garrow
Major's Mite of Daneend	Messrs. E. R. Porch & F. E. Todd
Reba Romance	Mrs. B. Anthony
Rodrick of Rushmoor	Miss V. M. Smith-Wood
Rooney of Rushmoor	Miss A. Wright
1932	
Clint Cheek	Mrs. B. Hewson
Columbine Cariad	Miss H. H. Shaw
Cooden Skypilot	Mr. R. W. Garrow
Danta of Daneend	Mr. R. W. Garrow
Placemore Prosperity	Mms. A. W. Bird & D. P. Allom
Skelum of the Roe	Mrs. E. M. Garnett
Wings	Miss P. Pacey
1933	
Bobby Bingo	Mrs. C. A. Hargreaves
Brean Taurie	Mrs. E. O. Innes
Carlin Rose	Mrs. B. Hewson

Name	*Owner*
Clint Topper	Mrs. B. Hewson
Leeside Larkspur	Mrs. F. Thornton
Wolvey Poacher	Mrs. C. Pacey
Wolvey Primrose	Mrs. C. Pacey

1934
Brean Glunyieman	Mrs. E. O. Innes
Columbine Cilean	Miss H. H. Shaw
Cooden Sheena	Mrs. O. R. Williams
Dude O'Petriburg	Mrs. A. Beels
Gwili Glendid	Mrs. M. N. Kidd
Leal Patricia	Miss M. Turnbull
Wolvey Peacock	Mrs. C. Pacey

1935
Brean Skelpie	Mrs. E. O. Innes
Calluna Clos	Miss A. A. Wright
Clint Chief	Mrs. B. Hewson
Jenifer	Mrs. M. Granville Ellis
Leal Phoenix	Miss M. Turnbull
Wolvey Pandora	Mrs. C. Pacey
Wolvey Poet	Mrs. C. Pacey

1936
Brean Lonnie	Mrs. E. O. Innes
Clint Constable	Mrs. B. Hewson
Rowenna of Rushmoor	Miss V. M. Smith-Wood
Wolvey Pintail	Mrs. C. Pacey
Wolvey Pongo	Mrs. C. Pacey
Wolvey Prefect	Mrs. C. Pacey

1937
Brean Gluclos	Mrs. E. O. Innes
Calluna Ruairidh	Miss A. A. Wright
Clint Cyrus	Mrs. B. Hewson
Columbine Cumanta	Miss H. H. Shaw
Throxenby Tempest	Mr. R. Fletcher
Wolvey Prophet	Mrs. C. Pacey

1938
Brean De Berri	Miss O. K. I. de Berry
Corrichie Cillmargo	Mr. B. Curickshank
Leal Flurry	Miss M. Turnbull
Leal Sterling	Miss M. Turnbull
MacEwan's Gift	Miss A. A. Wright
Misterdawson	Miss M. Davidson
Walfield Margaret	Miss O. K. I. de Berry
Wolvey Pattern	Mrs. C. Pacey
Wolvey Phantom	Mrs. C. Pacey
Wolvey Plainsman	Mrs. C. Pacey
Wolvey Playfellow	Mrs. C. Pacey

Name	*Owner*
1939	
MacSporran of Tiriosal	Mrs. C. MacKinnon Livey
Melbourn Mathias	Mr. F. Hewson
Robina of Rushmoor	Miss V. M. Smith-Wood
Rowberrow Rapture	Mrs. F. Thornton
Rowson of Rushmoor	Miss V. M. Smith-Wood

1947–62

Name	*Owners*	*Breeders*
1947		
Betty of Whitehills	Mrs. V. M. Swann	Mrs. F. E. Barr
Freshney Fiametta	Miss E. E. Wade	Mrs. M. McKinney
Shiningcliff Simon	Mrs. J. Finch	Mrs. J. Finch
Timoshenko of the Roe	Hon. Torfrida H. Rollo	Mrs. E. M. Garnett
1948		
Baffle of Branston	Mrs. D. M. Dennis	Mrs. D. M. Dennis
Pygmalion of Patterscourt	Mr. W. J. Patterson	Mr. W. J. Patterson
Hookwood Mentor	Miss E. E. Wade	Mr. A. Brown
Deidre of Kendrum	Hon. Torfrida H. Rollo	Hon. Torfrida H. Rollo
Cruben Crystal	Dr. & Mrs. A. Russell	Dr. & Mrs. A. Russell
Macairns Jemima	Mr. C. Drake	Mr. C. Drake
Wolvey Prospect	Mrs. C. Pacey	Mrs. C. Pacey
1949		
Athos of Whitehills	Mrs. V. M. Swann	Mrs. V. M. Swann
Binnie of Branston	Mrs. D. M. Dennis	Mrs. D. M. Dennis
Furzefield Pax	Mrs. D. P. Allom	Mrs. D. P. Allom
Heathcolne Freshney Flare	Mr. N. Baxter	Mrs. M. McKinney
Lorne Jock	Mr. N. A. MacEwan & Mr. A. McVicar	Mr. N. A. MacEwan & Mr. A. McVicar
Macconachie Tiena Joy	Mr. A. H. Salsbury	Mr. A. H. Salsbury
Shiningcliff Storm	Mr. H. S. Hallas	Mrs. J. Finch
Wolvey Penelope	Mrs. C. Pacey	Mrs. C. Pacey
Wolvey Prudence	Mrs. C. Pacey	Mrs. C. Pacey
1950		
Barrister of Branston	Mrs. D. M. Dennis	Mrs. D. M. Dennis
Brisk of Branston	Mrs. John G. Winant	Mrs. D. M. Dennis
Furzefield Preference	Miss E. E. Wade	Mrs. D. Allom
Heathcolne Roamer	Mrs. N. M. Baxter	Mrs. N. M. Baxter
Isla of Kendrum	Hon. Torfrida H. Rollo	Hon. Torfrida H. Rollo
Maree of Kendrum	Hon. Torfrida H. Rollo	Hon. Torfrida H. Rollo
Shiningcliff Sprig	Mrs. J. Finch	Mrs. J. Finch
1951		
Cruben Dextor	Dr. & Mrs. A. Russell	Dr. & Mrs. A. Russell
Crystone Chatterer	Mrs. E. Anthony	Mrs. E. Anthony
Crystone Cherry	Mrs. E. Anthony	Mrs. E. Anthony

Name	*Owners*	*Breeders*
Furzefield Provost	Mrs. D. P. Allom	Miss A. A. Wright
Hookwood Sensation	Miss E. E. Wade	Miss E. E. Wade
Lynwood Branston Blue	Mrs. G. Ellis	Mrs. D. M. Dennis
Mallaig Silver Empress	Miss E. E. Wade	Mr. E. Bagshaw
Mark of Old Trooper	Mr. E. Ward	Mr. E. Ward
Shiningcliff Snowcloud	Mrs. J. Finch	Mrs. J. Finch
Shiningcliff Sultan	Mrs. J. Finch.	Mrs. J. Finch
Staplands Shepherd	Mr. & Mrs. H. T. Walsh	Mr. & Mrs. H. T. Walsh
1952		
Cotsmor Crunch	Mrs. R. K. Capper	Mrs. R. K. Capper
Furzefield Pilgrim	Mrs. D. P. Allom	Mrs. D. P. Allom
Hasty Bits	Mrs. G. M. Barr	Mrs. G. M. Barr
Heathcolne Gowan	Mrs. F. M. Brownridge	Mrs. N. M. Baxter
Perchance of Patters-court	Mrs. R. Morgan-Jones	Mr. D. J. Patterson
Shiningcliff Dunthorne Damsel	Mrs. J. Finch	Mrs. J. Finch
Staplands Spitfire	Mr. & Mrs. H. T. Walsh	Mr. & Mrs. H. T. Walsh
Wolvey Piquet	Mrs. C. Pacey	Mrs. C. Pacey
Wolvey Poster	Mrs. C. Pacey	Mrs. C. Pacey
1953		
Calluna the Poacher	Mrs. A. Beels	Miss A. A. Wright
Cotsmor Cream Puff	Mrs. R. K. Capper	Mrs. R. K. Capper
Cruben Moray	Dr. & Mrs. A. Russell	Dr. & Mrs. A. Russell
Hookwood Gardenia	Mrs. G. M. Barr	Mr. H. Galt
Lynwood Blue Betty	Mr. & Mrs. G. Ellis	Mr. & Mrs. G. Ellis
Lynwood Timothy	Mr. & Mrs. G. Ellis	Mr. & Mrs. G. Ellis
Rosalan Rogue	Miss E. E. Wade	Miss E. E. Wade
Shiningcliff Donark Decision	Miss J. Finch.	Miss J. Finch
Shiningcliff Sugar Plum	Mrs. J. Finch	Mrs. G. Frost
Wolvey Peach	Mrs. C. Pacey	Mrs. C. Pacey
Wolvey Poppet	Mrs. C. Pacey	Mrs. C. Pacey
1954		
Bannock of Branston	Mrs. D. M. Dennis.	Mrs. D. M. Dennis
Biretta of Branston	Mrs. D. M. Dennis	Mrs. D. M. Dennis
Cotsmor Creambun	Mrs. R. K. Capper	Mrs. R. K. Capper
Eoghan of Kendrum	Hon. Torfrida H. Rollo	Hon. Torfrida H. Rollo
Famecheck Lucky Charm	Miss F. M. C. Cook	Miss F. M. C. Cook
Laird of Lochalan	Mrs. R. W. Scott	Mrs. R. W. Scott
Mairi of Kendrum	Miss J. H. Herbert	Hon. Torfrida H. Rollo
Tulyar of Trenean	Mrs. W. Dodgson	Mrs. W. Dodgson
Wolvey Pageboy	Mrs. C. Pacey	Mrs. C. Pacey
1955		
Brendalee	Mrs. H. M. Jeffrey	Mrs. H. M. Jeffrey
Famecheck Viking	Miss F. M. C. Cook	Miss F. M. C. Cook
Lynwood Marcia	Mr. & Mrs. G. Ellis	Mr. & Mrs. G. Ellis

Name	Owners	Breeders
1955—*cont.*		
Nice Fella of Wynsolot	Mrs. E. A. Green	Mrs. E. A. Green
Quakertown Quality	Mr. & Mrs. H. Sansom	Mr. & Mrs. H. Sansom
Raventofts Fuchsia	Mrs. N. Whitworth	Mrs. N. Whitworth
Rowmore Brora of Ken-nishead	Miss I. R. Maclean Cowie	Mrs. D. Wintersgill
Slitrig Solitaire	Mrs. C. M. Kirby	Mrs. C. M. Kirby
1956		
Banda of Branston	Mrs. D. M. Dennis	Mrs. D. M. Dennis
Bramhill Patricia	Mrs. J. H. Gee	Mrs. J. H. Gee
Famecheck Gay Crus-ader	Miss F. M. C. Cook	Miss F. M. C. Cook
Famecheck Happy Knight	Miss F. M. C. Cook	Miss F. M. C. Cook
Slitrig Shandy	Mrs. C. Pacey	Mrs. Kirby
Wolvey Patricia	Mrs. C. Pacey	Mrs. C. Pacey
Wolvey Philippa	Mrs. C. Pacey	Mrs. C. Pacey
Wolvey Pied Piper	Mrs. C. Pacey	Mrs. C. Pacey
1957		
Banker of Branston	Mrs. D. M. Dennis	Mrs. D. M. Dennis
Cruben Chilibean	Mr. & Mrs. A. Russell	Mr. & Mrs. A. Russell
Crystone Cressina	Mrs. E. Anthony	Mrs. E. Anthony
Famecheck Ballet Dancer	Mrs. G. Bingham	Miss F. M. C. Cook
Famecheck Comet	Mr. A. Berry	Miss F. M. C. Cook
Famecheck Lucky Mas-cot	Miss F. M. C. Cook	Miss F. M. C. Cook
Kirnbrae Symmetra Sailaway	Miss J. Brown	Mrs. V. R. Davidson
Mistymoor Andrea	Miss M. M. Batchelor	Miss M. M. Batchelor
Wolvey Pirate	Mrs. C. Pacey	Mrs. C. Pacey
1958		
Brindie of Branston	Mrs. D. M. Dennis	Mrs. D. M. Dennis
Calluna the Laird	Miss A. A. Wright	Miss A. A. Wright
Famecheck Gaiety Girl	Miss F. M. C. Cook	Miss F. M. C. Cook
Famecheck Lucky Choice	Miss F. M. C. Cook.	Miss F. M. C. Cook
Famecheck Lucky Roger	Mr. A. Berry	Miss F. M. C. Cook
Freshney Frey	Mrs. P. M. Welch	Mrs. M. McKinney
Quakertown Question-aire	Mrs. K. Sansom	Mr. & Mrs. H. Sansom
Riuelin Rustle	Mrs. M. W. Pearson	Mrs. M. Tazzyman
Shiningcliff Sheela	Mrs. J. Finch	Miss M. Holland
Sollershott Sun Up	Mrs. D. J. Kenney Taylor	Mrs. D. J. Kenney Taylor
Stoneygap Commodore	Mrs. G. M. Barr	Mrs. G. M. Barr
Wolvey Pipers Son	Mrs. C. Pacey	Mrs. C. Pacey
Wolvey Postmaster	Mrs. C. Pacey	Mrs. C. Pacey
1959		
Banessa of Branston	Mrs. D. M. Dennis	Mrs. D. M. Dennis

Name	Owners	Breeders
Bavena of Branston	Mrs. D. M. Dennis	Mrs. D. M. Dennis
Broomlaw Brandy	Mrs. M. Law	Mrs. M. Law
Citrus Warbler	Mrs. M. Lemon	Mrs. M. Lemon
Cruben Happy	Dr. & Mrs. A. Russell	Dr. & Mrs. A. Russell
Eriegael Mercedes	Miss J. Brown	Miss J. Brown
Famecheck Jolly Warrior	Miss F. M. C. Cook	Miss F. M. C. Cook
Furzefield Patrick	Mrs. D. P. Allom	Mrs. D. P. Allom
Phrana O'Petriburg	Mrs. A. Beels	Mrs. A. Beels
Wolvey Palor	Mrs. C. Pacey	Mrs. C. Pacey
Wolvey Pipers Tune	Mrs. C. Pacey	Mrs. C. Pacey
Wolvey Postgirl	Mrs. R. K. Mellon	Mrs. C. M. Kirby

1960

Name	Owners	Breeders
Bandsman of Branston	Mrs. D. M. Dennis	Mrs. D. M. Dennis
Broomheather Freesia	Mrs. E. Hay	Mrs. E. Hay
Eriegael Storm Child	Miss J. Brown	Miss J. Brown
Famecheck Gay Buccaneer	Miss F. M. C. Cook	Miss F. M. C. Cook
Famecheck Joy	Miss F. M. C. Cook	Miss F. M. C. Cook
Famecheck Musketeer	Miss F. M. C. Cook	Miss F. M. C. Cook
Glengyle Tapestry	Mrs. P. M. Welch	Miss P. M. Welch
Stoneygap Flash	Mrs. G. M. Barr	Mr. F. H. Hewett
Symmetra Skirmish	Miss J. Brown	Mr. & Mrs. H. Mitchell
Wolvey Pavlova	Mrs. C. Pacey	Mrs. C. Pacey
Wolvey Playgirl	Mrs. C. Pacey	Mrs. C. Pacey
Workman of Wynsolot	Mrs. E. A. Green	Mrs. E. A. Green

1961

Name	Owners	Breeders
Brenda of Branston	Mrs. D. M. Dennis	Mrs. D. M. Dennis
Broomheather Fleur de Lis	Mrs. E. Hay	Mrs. E. Hay
Buttons of Helmsleigh	Mrs. G. M. Barr	Mrs. S. R. Rowland
Glengyle Thistle	Mrs. P. M. Welch	Mrs. P. M. Welch
Phancy O'Petriburg	Mrs. A. Beels	Mr. & Mrs. L. A. Thomson
The Prior of Raventofts	Mrs. N. Whitworth	Mrs. N. Whitworth
Wolvey Permit	Mrs. C. Pacey	Mrs. C. Pacey
Wolvey Pickwick	Mrs. C. Pacey	Mrs. C. Pacey

1962

Name	Owners	Breeders
Banny of Branston	Mrs. D. M. Dennis	Mrs. D. M. Dennis
Birkfell Solitaire	Miss S. Cleland	Miss S. Cleland
Sollershott Soloist	Mrs. D. J. Kenney Taylor	Mrs. D. J. Kenney Taylor
Wolvey Punch	Mrs. C. Pacey	Mrs. C. Pacey

Specimen Pedigrees

1. PEDIGREE OF CH. WOLVEY POSTMASTER

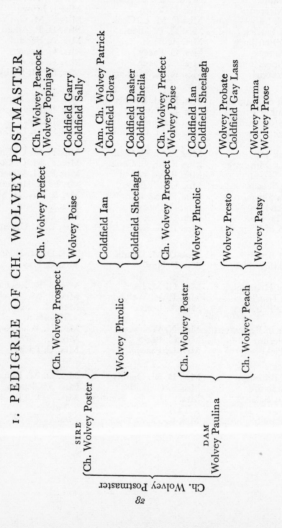

Ch. Wolvey Postmaster

SIRE
Ch. Wolvey Poster

DAM
Wolvey Paulina

Ch. Wolvey Prospect
Wolvey Phrolic
Ch. Wolvey Poster
Ch. Wolvey Peach

Ch. Wolvey Prefect
Wolvey Poise
Coldfield Ian
Coldfield Sheelagh
Ch. Wolvey Prospect
Wolvey Phrolic
Wolvey Presto
Wolvey Patsy

Ch. Wolvey Peacock
Wolvey Popinjay
Coldfield Garry
Coldfield Sally
Am. Ch. Wolvey Patrick
Coldfield Glora
Coldfield Dasher
Coldfield Sheila
Ch. Wolvey Prefect
Wolvey Poise
Coldfield Ian
Coldfield Sheelagh
Wolvey Probate
Coldfield Gay Lass
Wolvey Parma
Wolvey Prose

2. PEDIGREE OF CH. SHININGCLIFF SIMON

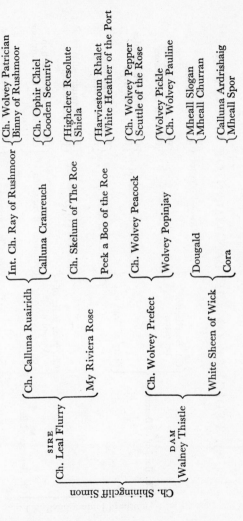

Ch. Shiningcliff Simon

SIRE
Ch. Leal Flurry

- Ch. Calluna Ruairidh
  - Int. Ch. Ray of Rushmoor
    - Ch. Wolvey Patrician
    - Binny of Rushmoor
  - Calluna Cranreuch
    - Ch. Ophir Chiel
    - Cooden Security
- My Riviera Rose
  - Ch. Skelum of The Roe
    - Highclere Resolute
    - Shiela
  - Peek a Boo of the Roe
    - Harviestoun Rhalet
    - White Heather of the Port

DAM
Walney Thistle

- Ch. Wolvey Prefect
  - Ch. Wolvey Peacock
    - Ch. Wolvey Pepper
    - Scuttle of the Rose
  - Wolvey Popinjay
    - Wolvey Pickle
    - Ch. Wolvey Pauline
- White Sheen of Wick
  - Dougald
    - Mheall Slogan
    - Mheall Churran
  - Cora
    - Calluna Ardrishaig
    - Mheall Spor

3. PEDIGREE OF CH. BANDSMAN OF BRANSTON

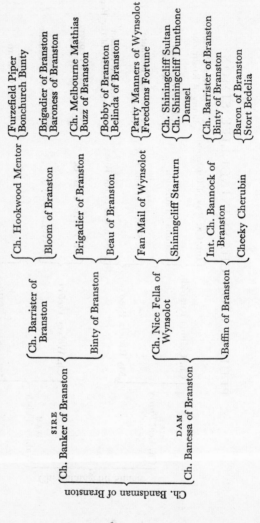

Ch. Bandsman of Branston

SIRE
Ch. Banker of Branston

Ch. Barrister of Branston

Ch. Hookwood Mentor
  Furzefield Piper
  Bonchurch Bunty

Bloom of Branston
  Brigadier of Branston
  Baroness of Branston

Binty of Branston

Brigadier of Branston
  Ch. Melbourne Mathias
  Buzz of Branston

Beau of Branston
  Bobby of Branston
  Belinda of Branston

DAM
Ch. Banessa of Branston

Ch. Nice Fella of Wynsolot

Fan Mail of Wynsolot
  Party Manners of Wynsolot
  Freedoms Fortune

Shiningcliff Starturn
  Ch. Shiningcliff Sultan
  Ch. Shiningcliff Dunthone
  Damsel

Baffin of Branston

Int. Ch. Bannock of Branston
  Ch. Barrister of Branston
  Binty of Branston

Cheeky Cherubin
  Baron of Branston
  Stort Bedelia

4. PEDIGREE OF FURZEFIELD PIPER

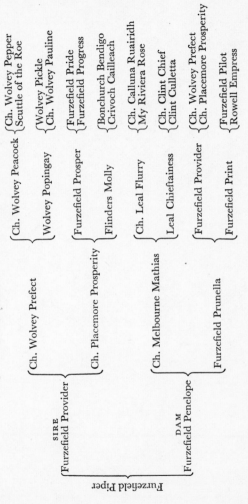

Furzefield Piper

SIRE
Furzefield Provider

Ch. Wolvey Prefect
- Ch. Wolvey Peacock
  - Ch. Wolvey Pepper
  - Scuttle of the Roe
- Wolvey Popingay
  - Wolvey Pickle
  - Ch. Wolvey Pauline

Ch. Placemore Prosperity
- Furzefield Prosper
  - Furzefield Pride
  - Furzefield Progress
- Flinders Molly
  - Bonchurch Bendigo
  - Crivoch Cailleach

DAM
Furzefield Penelope

Ch. Melbourne Mathias
- Ch. Leal Flurry
  - Ch. Calluna Ruairidh
  - My Riviera Rose
- Leal Chieftainess
  - Ch. Clint Chief
  - Clint Culletta

Furzefield Prunella
- Furzefield Provider
  - Ch. Wolvey Prefect
  - Ch. Placemore Prosperity
- Furzefield Print
  - Furzefield Pilot
  - Rowell Empress

INDEX

Index